SHIPWRECKED
INTERNATIONAL

SHIPWRECKED
INTERNATIONAL

DAVID SPEDDING

First published in 2001 by Channel 4 Books, an imprint of Pan Macmillan Ltd,
20 New Wharf Road, London N1 9RR, Basingstoke and Oxford.

Associated companies throughout the world.

www.panmacmillan.com

ISBN 0 7522 2024 1

Text © David Spedding, 2001

The right of David Spedding to be identified as the author of this
work has been asserted by him in accordance with the Copyright,
Designs and Patents Act 1988.

Cover photographs: top © Digital Vision; below © Channel 4 Books

All other photographs were taken by the *Shipwrecked* participants
© Channel 4 Books, 2001

9 8 7 6 5 4 3 2 1

A CIP catalogue record for this book is available from the British Library.

Designed and typeset by seagulls
Printed by Mackays of Chatham plc, Chatham, Kent

Acknowledgements: David Spedding would like to thank Frank Maloney,
Mark Frith, Emma Tait, Gillian Christie and Rob Dimery, with extra-special thanks
to all of the castaways for their amazing work and co-operation.

RDF MEDIA

This book accompanies the television series *Shipwrecked*,
made by RDFMedia.com for Channel 4.
Executive Producer: Shauna Minoprio
Series Producer: Eve Kay

CONTENTS

INTRODUCTION

There's a French expression, 'Jamais deux sans trois', which roughly translates as, 'If it works twice, it'll work a third time.' And sure enough, after two highly successful series, Channel 4's *Shipwrecked* has taken a third crew of willing castaways away from all the conveniences and luxuries of modern life, dispatched them to a beautiful tropical island, and invited us to sit back and watch how they coped with it all.

Of course, there can't be many people left in Britain who aren't already familiar with this particular Reality TV show. Having already seen two teams of young people survive the *Shipwrecked* experience, we've got a pretty good idea of how it works; we know pretty much what to expect, don't we? Er, guess again. Truth be told, we – much like this new batch of castaways – have no idea what's about to hit us.

See, there's another, more familiar French expression, 'Vive la différence', which translates (very loosely) as 'Repeating the same old same old is pretty boring.' And sure enough, the third chapter of the survival show is a very different beast to those that preceded it. The clue to the first significant change is in the title of this book. Long-term fans will recall that the first *Shipwrecked* was a very British affair, with all the castaways being UK residents. Series two sowed the seeds of change, when it unexpectedly thrust three Australians into the mix, but this version goes one step further, with a truly multi-national cast. Again, there are three

Australians joining in with the fun and games, but add to that a trio of Americans, one Sicilian and two French participants, and you've got a new, global flavour to the show, with more cultural differences flying around than ever before.

A total of sixteen castaways, then, would initially be marooned on the uninhabited South Pacific island of Yaukuvelevu, just south of Fiji. A larger island than has been previously used by *Shipwrecked*, and boasting 125 acres of wild terrain, Yaukuvelevu was the perfect environment, having its own natural water spring, and – crucially – plenty of natural food resources in the form of papaya, guava, breadfruit, mangoes and yams. Just a mile away lies the island of Dravuni, where the castaways would receive the training necessary for their stay before being despatched to Yaukuvelevu.

The first stage of the journey to tropical climes began in Britain – to be specific, in the heart of Surrey. The call for willing castaways had led to 25,000 people sending videotapes to production company RDF's offices, all begging for their chance to go to the island. From those, just fifty were invited to a selection weekend that would decide not just whether they were cut out for survival in extreme conditions, but also to ascertain that they could do so as part of a team. That decision would be made by a panel headed by T4's Andi Peters and two *Shipwrecked* producers, Eve Kay and David Frank.

Over three days, those fifty would be whittled down to just ten, the process commencing with each applicant being given sixty seconds to sell themselves to the panel. They rapped, they sang, they did handstands, they showed off their favourite underpants and one even brought along a chicken. But simply being wacky wasn't going to impress the panel – as Eve confirms, they were looking for that hard-to-define 'outstanding quality'. On the first day alone, twenty of the applicants returned home, having been judged to be lacking that 'X-factor'. The obvious attention-seekers bit the dust, as did the wallflowers, as did the applicant who confessed that he wouldn't be able to do the full ten-week stint, because it would mean him losing his job.

Those remaining were put through assault courses and team-work challenges; they were asked to improvise movie scenes together and they faced a series of brutally direct individual inter-views with the panel. On the second night, they camped out, constructing their own tents from tarpaulin and sticks, and feed-ing themselves on rabbits, which they were required to skin and gut for themselves. Interestingly, when it came to the grubby busi-ness of slitting open a bunny and removing its insides, it was the girls who took control while the lads contented themselves with congratulating them on a job well done.

As you'll see from the castaways' own accounts, the weekend was a remarkable time, with strong friendships rapidly being formed and, inevitably, irritating character traits already emerging. All told, it was an incredibly intense experience, but – as the successful applicants were warned by Andi Peters – the programme they would be appearing on was going to be infinitely more gruelling than anything they'd seen on *Shipwrecked* before.

Interestingly, it was one of the American crew who unwittingly pointed to the single biggest factor in the new regime, when she admitted that she'd seen very little of the previous series, but that she got the impression the show was 'kinda like MTV's *Real World*, only it's set on a beach'. You can see where she might get that idea, in fairness: think back to the two previous series and idyllic images of a sun-kissed paradise are the first memories to stir – lying on a beach, working on your tan, watching the sun rise over a calm sea… the perfect, picture-postcard holiday, really. Well, much as it pains us to shatter that beautiful image, the goalposts have been moved this time In fact, we're pretty much looking at an entirely different pitch, where one very simple alteration to the usual order of play turned heaven into hell.

The best illustration of that comes in a diary kept by one of the British castaways who, on arrival, wrote 'the beauty that immediately surrounded me made me feel so special'. However, a little further down, on the very same page, we see a very different mood emerging: 'I feel very depressed and sad. I'm beginning to miss home, but there's one thing I miss more than anything…' And the thing in question? Food. Whereas the two previous series saw the castaways receiving regular rations, *Shipwrecked* three provided the barest of necessities (cooking oil, salt and garlic), and left the group to pretty much fend for themselves. The expression that would come up again and again throughout the ten-week stay, and it's as fair a description of the circumstances as you'll find, was 'Hardcore survival'.

Of course, no one was going to be allowed to starve. Apart from the island's natural resources, a vegetable patch had been planted in advance of the group's arrival, and livestock had also been ferried in. And naturally, the castaways' health was closely monitored, with a doctor making regular visits to the island. But make no mistake, this was going to be infinitely harder than any of the previous outings, and whereas previous crews had complained of their endlessly bland diet of rice, rice and more rice, this lot soon came to view those fluffy white grains as the finest delicacy available to the human palate.

The next difference was one that could have arisen at any time since the series first started. Until now, no one had really been aware of the existence of an Island Constitution, largely because no one had ever needed to refer to it. But it's always been there – a sort of community rule-book, if you will, one that provides the castaways with a form of social justice and the power to deal with any problems they might have with certain members of the team. More specifically, it allows a majority vote to expel people from the island.

Now, for various reasons, the previous two series had seen people opting out of the programme before it reached its end, and *Shipwrecked* series three is no different in that regard. People departed, people arrived halfway through, all sorts of chopping and changing went on throughout, but the biggest shock came when the castaways decided to expel one of their own from the island. A momentous decision, and one that wasn't taken lightly, but one that would reverberate through their community long after that person had left...

Over the following pages, you'll get to meet each and every one of the castaways, share their experiences and hear their stories. And they certainly have some tales to tell. Each of them faithfully kept a diary while on the island, documenting all the highs and lows of the experience, their personal thoughts, the stuff that happened when the camera wasn't looking, who they hated, who they liked, who they fancied, who they didn't. For the most part, these diaries served almost as a form of therapy, a chance to get away from the group and make sense of everything that was happening. You'll see people go through the most extraordinary changes, survive quite unbelievable brushes with the harsher elements of life, and just as importantly, you'll find yourself getting closer to them than you'd think possible.

One thing all the castaways agree on is that you can't really begin to understand what it was like unless you were actually there on the island. When you read about what happened to them out there, you'll see that this is no idle boast – but thanks to the honesty of those diaries, you'll get pretty damn close. You'll also meet a team of people who have endured an experience most of us would never be able to cope with. For that much, you can only respect them – they've certainly earned it.

1

GENEVIEVE
CLAUDI

Age: 24
Profession: Full-time carer
Luxury Item: Tobacco

Genevieve had watched every episode of the first two *Shipwrecked* series and swore to herself that she would apply for the next one. 'I watched the programmes, and I really wanted to be there,' she confessed, before setting off. 'I'm one hundred per cent confident that I can do it,' she added. 'The selection weekend showed me that. A lot of people came feeling very sure of themselves, but they were wrong.'

French-born Genevieve has lived in London for five years now, and has one of those adorable, gentle accents and an impossibly infectious laugh. That said, and as she's the first to admit, she's no pushover. 'But I'm not the dominant type,' she stresses. 'I'm not like that. I'm very patient. If I've got something to say, I will let people know what I'm thinking straight away, but I'm not a bully.'

Moreover, in a revelation that was bound to make her popular among the castaways, she announced well in advance that she wanted to do all the washing up on the island. 'That will give me fifteen minutes to myself every day,' she explained, 'just to think about other things. I like to do washing up, I really do.' Asked why she thought she had been selected, she says, 'Well, I adapt very quickly to things, and I work well with people. I love talking to people. Not being the centre of attention, don't get me wrong — I'm very easy-going, and I just love talking to people.'

That ability to adapt would be tested on arrival at Yaukuvelevu, when the new, hardcore regime characteristic of this series became clear. 'I was shocked,' she admits, 'but I was also very excited — I had no idea what to expect, but I was pleased, to be honest with you. The island was an amazing place — absolutely fantastic. And I was happy that they were giving us a challenge. Everyone was suffering, but I felt really pleased with myself — I thought, right, this is hard, but we're here on a beautiful island paradise, and I'm going to make the best of it. But there is no doubt — this experience is going to change everyone's lives.'

That enthusiastic determination wasn't immediately shared by all, and Genevieve quickly noticed that not everyone was coping so well. 'Vicki is hungry, tired, hot and very bad all round — she can't sleep either,' she wrote in her diary, 'but we're all discovering what it is really like to live like a Fijian. I feel tired too,' she admitted, 'and I have terrible munchies, but Salvo's making me laugh a lot.'

From the outset, there seemed to be a bond between Salvo and Genevieve. The larger-than-life Sicilian was the kind of guy who inspired the most mixed of emotions, from 'infuriation' to 'adoration'. 'We were always together,' Genevieve recalls. 'People had already started to get annoyed with him, and nobody was really talking to him. He was very loud, and some people couldn't take it. It's nice when someone comes along and makes you laugh for half an hour, sure, but with Salvo it just became too much. So he turned to me for friendship, and we became very good friends.'

When the group took the decision to treat themselves to two of the chickens that had been provided for them, it was Salvo who took charge of the killing, while Genevieve busied herself with the preparation. She was clearly impressed by Salvo's survival instinct:

> He's a great help on the island. A very strong man — a jungle-man with a big heart. He killed the two chickens with his bare hands, broke their necks and then slashed their throats. It had been a long time since I gutted and boned a chicken — the last time was when I was in North Africa many years ago. But I did enjoy it, don't get me wrong!

In those early days, the mood of the group fluctuated wildly from one day to the next. As Genevieve explained in her diary, 'Everyone thought it would be just like the last series, but oh no, it has been very hard training for all of us. For the first week we ate the same food every day; and everyone is so hungry. But I do believe if we stay together and help each other, we'll be fine. It's surprising how life can turn around...'

It certainly is. One surprise in particular came sooner than Genevieve could have expected. And the turnaround was one that she'd never predicted, one that still leaves her feeling shocked and angry. It began with the arrival on Day 3 of six more castaways, three Australians and three Americans. 'At the beginning, everyone was together, happy with each other,' she frowns, 'but then the Australians and Americans arrived and things started to change. The day they came, we were very happy that they'd arrived. But then the guys started to all group together, and making differences between them and the girls. It became quite sexist, definitely.'

The new arrivals also seemed to have a marked effect on Genevieve's friendship with Salvo:

> Until then he'd been with me for twenty-four hours a day. One day we were friends, the next he turned his back on

me. Just like that, no explanation, not even a word. I didn't understand the way he just changed. I think it was because the Australians had arrived, and that was it – he'd found his new mate, Leon. He became a very different Salvo from the one I'd known until then. Actually, he showed the true Salvo when he changed. The Salvo we'd seen in the beginning wasn't the real person.

But for Genevieve, the problem didn't just lie with Salvo. 'It's a shame,' she said, on her return to England. 'Everyone was so pleased to be there, and everyone should have been helping each other. The thing was, all the guys started to turn on the girls, complaining that they weren't doing their jobs. But I was the only one of the girls who would stand up to the boys. I'd say, "Listen you can't talk to us like this, you've got no right. We're all in the same boat, you're a man, you're supposed to be stronger, so why don't you help instead of criticizing? Show us what to do."'

Then, on Day 11, what seemed like a relatively minor matter provoked a falling-out that would, in due course, change the history of *Shipwrecked*. Genevieve recalls the evening all too well:

Malia and Salvo were cooking breadfruit with these green leaves. Me and Sarah-Jane said we didn't want the leaves, and could they leave some breadfruit on the side for us to eat? So Malia and Leon started complaining, saying, 'Why should you be allowed to have a treat?' I said, 'What's the problem? I don't want to eat those leaves, I just want to eat the breadfruit.' Then we asked if we could have just a little bit of oil so we could fry it, and Simon, Salvo, Geordie and Randy started joining in complaining – you can imagine the picture. Everybody shouting, saying 'No, you can't have any oil.' So I asked Leon to sort it out, since he was leader, and nothing was being discussed, it was all just shouting. And he was saying, 'Well, I'm sorry, if no one's happy then you can't have the oil.' So that was it, we forgot about the oil and made breadfruit soup. But I was very hurt. The boys spoke to me in a very bad way, and I don't forget things like that.'

The upshot of this argument was that the following day, Genevieve, Vicki, Sarah-Jane, Gemma and Donna decided to form their own separate group, aiming to set up their own camp in a different area of the island. Naturally, they would need provisions, and events started to get a little out of hand... Waiting for the others to leave the camp area, the girls took advantage of their absence to help themselves to some pots and pans, and a share of the basic provisions that had been supplied. The problem was, they didn't announce their intentions to any of the other castaways, so when the items were discovered to be missing, the obvious conclusion that people leaped to was that there was a thief among them.

Shawn, having witnessed some of the girl's actions, confirmed that it had been a group effort, but as the others started discussing what had happened, Genevieve's name came up more than anyone else's. Everyone, it seemed, had some story of her either trying to steal something, or encouraging others to steal things with her. It's worth noting that none of them had actually *seen* her commit any of the acts she was suddenly being accused of, but there was a lot of putting two and two together going on.

Asked why she thinks she was singled out like this, Genevieve offers the following theory: 'I was always stepping in and speaking my mind – I'm a very straightforward person. If I like you, I'll tell you so, if I don't like you, I'll tell you that straight away too. I don't like hypocrites. So I was always there, standing up for the girls. And the guys didn't like that – it was too much for them.' The crunch moment, for her, had been the start of Week 2, when Leon was elected leader. 'Of course, he was leader of the whole group,' she says, 'but he only seemed interested in being leader of the guys.'

This view was pretty much born out by Jeffro's comments: 'That whole problem was Leon's fault in a way,' he confirms. 'He desperately wanted to be leader in the second week, and no one else was interested in doing it, basically – and he did try and make it like some kind of dictatorship. Wanted to make his own mark, I think, and I really don't think Genevieve would have had this trouble if it hadn't been for him. It did upset me that Leon and Salvo had so much influence – and that was only because they had the biggest mouths on them.'

There was already a sense of scapegoats being searched for, and Genevieve was well aware of it:

Although I wasn't voted in as a leader, in a way they saw me as the girls' leader. And then it started, with all the talking behind my back. The girls and I used to go over to the other side of the island, having fun together, laughing together, not paying any attention to the boys. So the boys started wondering what we were doing, and because they didn't actually know, they just started making up stories – it was like being back at school, really. It was mad.

The stories read, to an outsider, like a tally of thoroughly petty accusations. In fairness, it's worth remembering that any source of nutrition was worth its weight in gold to the castaways – it was vital to conserve what little they had for the entire ten-week stay. So when it appeared (and appearances are pretty much all we have to go by) that someone was dipping into those resources, it was plainly a rather bigger deal for the people who would have to go without.

Malia, for example, had come across a freshly discarded papaya skin at the end of the first week, and was now claiming that

Genevieve had tried to interest her in stealing some more. Geordie, for his part, had suspected Genevieve of stealing soy sauce to add to her breadfruit broth – something she'd denied, although he tasted the slops in her bowl afterwards and confirmed that she'd used soy to liven up the impossibly bland soup. Matches had been discovered on the beach, and with Genevieve being a smoker, the finger had been pointed at her.

A meeting was duly called, and as Genevieve explains:

It was astonishing. Everyone was on their high horse, no one was listening to anyone else. Things were said, questions were thrown at me, and I just laughed. Because the things they were saying weren't true. And that just made them even more angry. Then, in front of the camera, Geordie says, 'Can I ask you a question? Do you respect me?' And as soon as he said that, I just started laughing. He thought I was going to give him a straight answer, but he hadn't respected *me* the night before, so I just asked him if he respected me. And that was it. Everybody became heated, and the guys all hated me, and they decided they wanted me off the island.

In fairness, when faced with a bunch of angry people, it's perhaps not the most diplomatic of moves to laugh at them, whether they're right or wrong. As Jeffro would later confirm, 'Genevieve got so many people's backs up. She annoyed me so much in that meeting. The thing is, she could have stuck up for herself, but she just gave in and started crying.'

It might come as a surprise to many viewers, but the *Shipwrecked* constitution *does* allow the group to vote one of their own to be taken off the island. In the previous two series that sanction hadn't been used, but with everyone convinced – whatever their reasoning – that Genevieve was stealing from the group, Allan, Salvo and Randy made a trip to HutCam to make the necessary nomination. As Allan explains, 'I was one of the people involved in the nomination, even though she hadn't stolen anything from me. In a situation like that, you just have to be ultra-fair. Everything has to be one hundred per cent, no grey areas. When we asked her about the thefts, my reaction was one of complete incredulity – I couldn't believe that she wouldn't admit that she'd done it, even though there were eight people saying that she had. Eight people aren't going to sit there and lie.'

Genevieve, for her part, was unaware that this was happening:

> The girls and I had gone to the beach to talk about what had gone on at the meeting. I said, 'I've got a feeling that something is going to happen. Something big.' And at that moment the whistle went, and we knew that something was going on. So we went to the camp, and Leon says that they are having a vote to take me off the island. And – boom – I was lost for words. I couldn't speak. I was thinking in French, thinking 'What is happening? This isn't possible.' I was just in a state of total shock. It was like the lunatics had taken over the asylum. Basically, the girls liked me, but the guys didn't, and Leon wanted to use that opportunity to throw me out.

An anonymous vote showed that eight of the castaways wanted Genevieve to go, five wished her to stay, and two had abstained. According to the terms of the constitution, she would have to leave Yaukuvelevu the next morning at 7.00am. She would spend her last night on the beach with the girls, before being collected by boat the following day.

The expulsion was an extraordinary event, one that would continue to reverberate throughout the remainder of the other castaways' time on the island. And while it may seem, if not unjust, then at the very least harsh to us, Allan was quick to explain the context:

> Until you're out there you can't fully understand what it was like. The flipside to that is that it's hard to make people back home understand. What she did was lots of little things that just got under all our skins, and built up to a point where it exploded. Back home, you explain it to your friends, saying, 'Well she stole a papaya, she stole matches, she stole a cigarette' and they say 'Yeah?' – it just doesn't seem very important. But out there, when you're trying to do something as a group, you can't have someone undermining everything. It wasn't just the fact that she was stealing, it was the fact that she was also trying to get others to do the same. It was quite a split group at the time. She was hanging around with the English girls, and the rest of us took this decision to vote her off without telling them. We had enough votes to chuck her off anyway. But even then, she'd been stealing off the English girls as well – she took some of Sarah-Jane's hot chocolate without asking her.

Chloe-Jane, who – for what it's worth – had also taken some of Sarah-Jane's hot chocolate without asking her, remains firm in her view that the action, while regrettable, was one that ultimately helped the group:

> I've thought about how truly devastating it must be for one person to lose such an opportunity, but at the time you can only go by your instinct. I was one of the ones who voted her off, and after discussing it with the others, we came to the conclusion that it was the best decision for the good of

the group. At that stage of our progress, that was what we had to do to enable us to carry on. I was sat on the boat with Geordie one day, and we got on to the subject of Genevieve and we came to the opinion that we just didn't trust her at all. She is quite a devious little character – there was always something that she was up to. And for her own personal gain. She was leading the English girls to one side and they were following her like sheep. The girls all stood up for her at the meeting, but basically Genevieve had insti-gated the whole thing.

Some, then, stood very much by the view that they'd done the right thing in difficult circumstances. Others, however, were rather less certain, as Jeffro explains:

I was really trying to keep a realistic head on, which was the complete opposite to what Salvo and Leon were doing. It was a shock to a lot of us, and it really wasn't planned. It went a bit far when people were singing 'Genevieve, profes-sional thief,' that's the biggest slap in the face. And I'm so ashamed, but I threw in a verse myself. But I've got a clear conscience about it – I voted no: I didn't agree with taking anyone's experience away from them. People asked me why I wasn't voting her off, and I just said, 'Think about when this goes out on television – she's going to be made out to be a thief, and all her friends are going to be watching it. Just to think that her neighbours are going to be watching her thrown off for stealing, seeing her being disgraced. People just didn't think about the consequences.

It would be a further five days before Genevieve was able to get a flight back to London, but she recalls those five days in Fiji as being particularly happy ones. 'The programme makers were fantastic to me,' she smiles. 'They really looked after me. One of them even wrote a song about me, which was fantastic – I have to be happy about that!'

That said, she was constantly aware that fifteen other young people were enjoying the experience that had just been taken away from her. 'I was gutted, to be honest. But like my mother told me, "You can never trust anyone but yourself."'

And when she was back in London, a cruel twist of fate meant that she was in time to see the repeated second series of *Shipwrecked* on Channel 4. 'It really hurt,' she admits. 'I really wanted to be there, that's why I applied! I wanted to be there from Day 1, right through to the end. I was one hundred per cent up to it, and I wanted to enjoy every single second of it. That last day on Yaukuvelevu, I wanted to chain myself to a tree and stay. It was such a beautiful place,' she sighs, 'but when I think of some of the people... to hear how they were manipulating everything I said, to hear my words being twisted, it was just weird. I don't know, maybe the sun was too hot for some people there... I'll tell you one thing, though, there were a lot of insecure people there. I was too confident for some of them.'

Understandably enough, Genevieve remains very angry about the incident. 'I will never forget and I will never forgive,' she says firmly. 'Never. I know that justice will be done, though, the truth will come out, and I'm a great believer in karma. I know I'm going to see these people again, and I'll speak to the ones who I liked, but as far as the others are concerned, I never want to see them again.'

2

GEORGE 'GEORDIE' TAYLOR

Age: 22 (21 on arrival at island)
Profession: 'Jackaroo' (Translation: farm labourer)
Luxury Item: Guitar

Geordie Taylor had never even left Australia before setting off for Yaukuvelevu. His first overseas jaunt, then, was set to be a memorable one... Speaking before the event, he was understandably excited. 'It's going to be an awesome experience,' he gushed. 'Firstly, just getting away from Australia. And secondly, the whole idea of the show really appeals to me – that "fending for yourself" aspect. When they told us it was going to be harder [than it had been for the show's previous castaways], that just put a huge grin on my face – I'm all for it. I just can't wait to discover this place.'

Now, the American and Australian contingent arrived on Yaukuvelevu on Day 3. By which time, well, it's fair to say that things were not looking too clever. 'It was a pretty amazing experience just arriving there,' recalls Geordie. 'Completely insane, in fact. It was just so incredible to see the island, for starters – it was such a rugged-looking place. And when we met the others, it was just crazy – everything was up in the air and no one really had much of an idea about food. You got the impression that no one had really taken control, even though Chloe-Jane had been elected leader. It was all pretty laid-back…'

As the castaways' diaries confirmed, the arrival of the international contingent gave the original group a feeling akin to that of being rescued. Although Geordie was the only member of that group with a rural background, it soon became clear that the Aussies and Americans were a little better prepared for life in the rough than the Brits:

> It really was very clear pretty much straight away that we were much more comfortable in that environment. The thing is, in Australia we're much closer to the bush – even when you're in a city it's never that far away. Leon and Malia had done their fair bit of camping already, and I'm from the outback anyway. I mean, the Brits killed two chickens on their first night – we still had seventy nights to go, and only twenty-eight chickens left, so that kind of summed it up for me. Maybe it was just excitement – those first hours on the island were pretty strange for everyone.

As Geordie had pointed out before setting off, his survival skills were as solid as you could wish for. 'I've done a lot of bushwalking, camping and fishing,' he explained, 'and I can kill a sheep, and prepare it to eat.' That last skill would soon be called upon when, on Day 9, the hungry castaways made the decision to kill one of the pigs. As it transpired, it would be Salvo who dealt the fatal blow, but the memory of the experience still troubles Geordie. 'Mate, I've seen everything when it comes to killing animals,' he sighs, 'but that was just so hard in so many ways. It was never going to be easy – you know, if we'd had a gun we could have just shot it and that would be it, done. But what could we do?'

He worries even now that the footage will show the castaways to be blood-crazed lunatics, although the scene – while incredibly hard to watch – makes it clear that these were necessary choices being made. 'It makes us look bad, I'm sure,' he insists. 'But really, it was so hard, and Salvo was incredibly brave to do that – the last thing I would have wanted to do was knife a pig on camera. Killing animals was a huge issue throughout the show, and I know Malia got very upset about it. My auntie's a vegetarian, actually, and when she sees that she'll hate it – she probably won't talk to me for a couple of weeks.'

It was one of the other Australians, Leon, who first assumed the position of leader elect, although few envied him that task in the second week, given that it meant dealing with Genevieve's expulsion. At a time when this working community needed to establish itself, there were large-scale distractions and tempers were high, a situation that didn't immediately improve when Genevieve departed. As Week 3 started, Geordie had already established himself as a hugely popular member of the team and was accordingly elected leader.

'Leon had had a really tough week as leader with the whole Genevieve business,' recalls Geordie, 'so my main push when I was elected was to try and get the group to have some fun – you know, get them to realize that that was what we came there for.' In keeping with this game plan, Geordie's first act on being elected leader was to thank the castaways, before launching into his performing seal impersonation.

That said, there was still a need for organization. Leon had managed to alienate some members of the team and it was now down to Geordie to try to mend some of the bridges:

> I put forward the idea that if we could all put in two hours' work every day, it would just make everything a lot smoother for everyone. Unfortunately, as a leader I didn't

enforce that and it never really happened. A lot of it was due to my lack of energy, though – in those circumstances you don't really feel like pushing people or jumping up and down about things. It was important to get everyone pulling together, but even in that third week, there were still a few people doing everyone else's work, and it got kind of frustrating. And then to cap it all, Gemma and Donna decided to leave, so that just threw everything I'd planned – I really wanted my week as leader to be the one in which everyone found their feet and worked out what they were there for. I'd actually approached all the British girls and said that if anything was ever bothering them that they should come and talk to me about it, because I was having a really good time and I wanted everyone else to. But it wasn't their cup of tea, I guess.

As far as 'working out what you're here for' goes, Geordie had known all along what his motivation was. 'Initially, I never went for the exposure,' he grins. 'All I wanted to do was go to this island and do some fishing.' Ah yes, fishing. Some of the Brits had already announced that they were less than keen on eating fish prior to arriving on Yaukuvelevu, but after a few days of meagre portions of yam and breadfruit, the prospect of fresh fish straight from the Pacific was beginning to sound very attractive. Armed with a simple rod, Geordie took himself out to see what he could catch for the group. And returned with nothing. Which was disheartening, sure, but it didn't put him off trying again the next day. And, again, returning with no fish.

What went wrong? I'd say I was definitely in the wrong spot. I just had it in my head that all I had to do was chuck a line in, and wherever I chose I was bound to catch some fish. I mean, this was the Tropics, after all. By the end of the stay I was catching fish, and I knew where to go, but in those first ten days of flat-out fishing, I was in the wrong spot and I should really have tried somewhere new every day. And yeah, it was demoralizing. I've never had problems catching fish anywhere else!

Geordie had constructed his own shelter right by the beach and would sleep in the sand quite happily. As he wrote in his diary, 'When I wake in the morning I shake sand out of my hair, I have sand in my sleeping bag, sand *everywhere* basically, but I don't mind – waking up on that beach is the best feeling in the world.' With those highs came the lows, though, and as would so often be the case, they were generally attributable to the lack of food. In another diary entry, Geordie wrote, 'I never want to forget how hungry I was today. One day I will probably laugh about it, but I hope I don't. All I know is that I'm a very lucky person to be able to eat what I want when I'm at home – it's only now that I've come to appreciate that not many people in the world have that luxury.'

That said, the picture of Geordie that emerges from the others' comments is one of a happy-go-lucky guy who didn't let things get him down, and could see the positive in any situation, however desperate it might seem. Ask him why he kept his darker moments to himself and he simply shrugs:

That's just me. When I was feeling low, I'd maybe discuss it with Malia or Leon, or anyone else close to home. The thing is, no one's perfect and there's no point in criticizing people out there, it just makes matters worse for everyone. So that was what I tried to stick to – you know, keep your thoughts to yourself and if you don't like something, then try to work around it, don't get caught up in other people's problems. So yeah, I had some low points, but looking back, I don't know how I let anything bother me – it was such an amazing place. I miss it so much.

In any situation in life, you always have your good and your bad, but in a situation like that, where everyone's stressed, and hungry and tired, it's just so much clearer, it becomes more and more obvious. But you only really remember the good things. I saw the second series of *Shipwrecked*, and I distinctly remember someone saying that you get the highest of highs and the lowest of lows, and that sums the experience up perfectly.

On the list of highs, Geordie would immediately single out 25 June, the day of his birthday:

That was definitely one of the highlights of the trip for me. For the party, we all decided to dress up. Which was no easy task, given what we had out there. Malia made me this huge top hat out of leaves, and I wore a cardboard bow tie. We had that big bamboo table, all dressed up, and everyone sitting around it looked so good. By that point we'd all lost a heap of weight, we were all nicely tanned and everything. And the others all put in loads of effort – I saved a bottle of rum and we had a massive bowl of coconut milk with rum and lemons in it. I don't think anyone got really drunk, but Chloe-Jane managed to get fairly merry, I seem to recall. Compared to some of the other parties, it was a fairly sober affair, actually, but everyone had a fantastic time. Salvo made this awesome cake with my name written out in fruit on it. I remember just sitting at the head of the table, grinning. I actually got given a book of 'Happy Birthday' letters from all the others, and it's just the nicest present I've ever had – everyone was just so generous in what they said. I've never felt so important.

Other highlights inevitably fall under the 'you had to be there' category, the kind of feelgood moments inspired by events that might seem ordinary, but which mattered enormously to the individual. For Geordie, such a moment arrived when he caught his first fish, just four days after his birthday. 'At last!' he wrote in his diary:

One fresh fish on the line! Nice big mackerel, about 8 pounds. Am *so* happy. Salvo cooked some bread to go with it and we had a great curry dipping sauce to go with it. It's great to have a full stomach. Actually, I've been feeling pretty good these last few days. I will miss this island, but I know I will step off it a better man. I don't know exactly *how* yet, but I do know that nothing as hard as surviving here comes without reward. Every one of these people drives me mad at times, but every one of them is also a friend whom I respect and trust. It's great to have people from the other side of the world sleeping down on the beach with you, cooking you bread, telling you stories, making you laugh. I'm lucky.

Whereas many of the castaways firmly insisted that they had no regrets about their time on the island, Geordie did. 'I hate to say it, but I really wish I'd done more out there,' he reflected, on his return to Australia. 'You fall into the trap of being lethargic, and I think a lot of that was to do with being short of food, but there were so many things I talked about doing and never got around to achieving. Like making a really good boat to do some island-hopping on, or the irrigation system for the veggie garden. And that would have worked for sure.' His diary backs this up, with page after page of detailed plans (including the aforementioned irrigation system, to be constructed out of bamboo canals) of improvements Geordie wanted to make to the island. You get the feeling that had they forgotten to collect the castaways at the end of the ten weeks, not only would he have coped rather well with a continued stay on Yaukuvelevu, but he'd have been happy to have remained shipwrecked:

> Oh, totally. I know I keep going on about it, but the beauty of the place was amazing. Like nothing you've ever encountered. In the last ten days, when we all chilled out a bit, I swam with dolphins and a manta ray. That ray was about 9 or 10 feet across. I just swam out and was bobbing about in the ocean, and the next thing I knew this ray just popped up underneath me. It flapped its huge wings and turned side-on to get a good look at me. I tried to swim closer, but it just took off gracefully toward the bottom of the ocean. A real once-in-a-lifetime moment.

Like all the other members of the team, Geordie voluntarily holds his hand up to an act of theft (remembering that 'theft' in this community meant 'failing to share all food with all the others') before the ten weeks were through, and, appropriately enough for this keen fisherman, it involved seafood. Just four days before the end of the stay, Geordie and Salvo went night-fishing and returned with a good haul of red snapper. As Geordie wrote in his diary, 'We walked back to camp, sat down and cooked our fish over the fire. Salvo and I ate it with huge grins on our faces. I wanted to share it, but it was great to be king for a day, and I had never eaten anything before without sharing it with the rest of the group. Didn't feel too guilty with only four days left!'

When the time finally came to leave Yaukuvelevu, Geordie celebrated his departure – as you do – with a quick streak through what was left of the camp, before returning to the civilized world. But if at that point he thought he'd finished with television shows, he was soon to be proven very wrong

I got on the plane back, and this good-looking Australian girl came up to me and said, 'Do you by any chance know who's been evicted from *Big Brother* this week?' And the whole bloody plane was talking about it all the way home, and I'd just got off this desert island and I had no *idea* what was going on. It soon turned out that *Big Brother* had been *huge* in Australia, and had really gripped the whole country. But I watched a bit of it and I thought I would never have lasted in that environment.

Given the fact that the subject of food had been such major part of life on Yaukuvelevu, it makes a certain kind of sense that Geordie's next brush with modern life involved the quest for something to eat:

Malia and I were on a flight together, and we were just eating and boozing flat out. And at the airport I tried to get some crisps out of this vending machine, but they got stuck. So there I was, wearing a sarong, in front of 400 passengers, trying to shake the crisps out of this machine, lifting it off the ground. I must have looked completely freaky. My dad took a picture of the two of us getting off the plane, and it really sums it up. We were both just laughing so much, so happy to be back.

The return to Australia left Geordie little time to even think about the experience he'd just survived. 'I started work sheep-shearing pretty much as soon as I got back,' he explains, 'so I didn't really have time to think about how different things were. I mean, I felt pretty weird at times; there were certainly some moments at parties when I just didn't want to be there and had to get out and get some fresh air. Early one morning, Emma – my girlfriend – found me sitting cross-legged watching TV, looking completely perplexed, you know, "Wow, look at the TV." You find it a bit hard to be in confined spaces, definitely. Other than that, she's not really noticed many differences in me.'

But there's little doubt that his ten-week stint as a castaway has left an indelible mark on young Geordie. 'It was amazing,' he enthuses, 'I don't know how I'm going to top it. Having a whole island to yourself, and being able to do whatever you want every day, is so far removed from what I'm used to.'

And having finally had his first overseas trip at the age of twenty-one, Geordie's already looking forward to his next one. 'Oh yes, I've got big plans,' he says.' Hopefully I'm going to come over to London and visit everyone who was out there with me. But I don't see how I'm ever going to top the experience of being on that island. I'll tell you one thing, though, after seeing the difference between the last series and this one, well, you've just gotta feel sorry for the people who go on the fourth series, really.'

3

GEMMA
POND

Age: 19
Profession: British Airways PR
Luxury Item: A hammock

If Genevieve had the best laugh on the island, then the prize for the most dazzling smile went, without any doubt, to Gemma. The sad thing was that even by her own admission, Gemma found little to smile about for much of her stay. Like so many of the other British castaways, she was already very familiar with *Shipwrecked*, and even remembered getting caught up in the selection special for series two: 'I watched the programme and I remember thinking "Why are you crying? You've known these people all of five minutes."'

She got the answer to that question first-hand when Channel 4 invited her to the selection weekend for series three:

I swear, there was so much emotion in the air. Everyone was on a high one moment, down in the dumps the next. You've got so many emotions running through you. A lot of it's down to nerves – it really is quite nerve-racking when it comes to the elimination. You're all in the same boat, and then when people you like are told they're not going, it's really sad. I never cry normally, but even I got quite tearful.

The other surprise for Gemma that weekend was finding out how quickly you can change your original assessment of the people around you. 'There were people that you thought, "Yeah, I could get on with them quite well," but then as more of their personality came across, you realized you were probably quite wrong with your first instinct. There's a lot of people going who I got on well with at the weekend, though,' she said before leaving England. 'If people I didn't like had gotten through, then I don't actually think I would have gone at all.'

The idea of being on television appealed to Gemma, sure, but she never viewed *Shipwrecked* as a potential career springboard: 'As far as I'm concerned, it's a real chance to discover just how much you take for granted,' she predicted. 'I don't think I appreciate what I have. Actually, a lot of people don't think I'm going to last five minutes, but I'm going to prove to myself and to everyone else that I can do this – I think that will just make me appreciate a lot of things.'

On arrival at Yaukuvelevu, though, she soon realized that no amount of preparatory *Shipwrecked*-viewing could have prepared her for what they were facing:

You look at the first two series and it looks like a piece of piss! All those people lying around getting suntans – and that's what I thought it would be like, if I'm honest. Sadly, I was wrong: it was totally not what we were expecting – we were assuming there'd be rice and tins of corned beef and all that, and there was *nothing* like that. For the first day or so we all still thought we were going to stumble across some rations or something, and that was the real reason that we were exploring the island so thoroughly – then after a few days it sort of sunk in: there wasn't going to be any rice or tins, and the only food we had was the vegetable patch that we'd found on the first day, and that was non-existent at that point. Oh yes, there were two pigs and a bunch of chickens as well. So you can imagine us lot – distraught, devastated, absolutely starving and all of us close to tears. I don't think a single one of us was happy. It was all a major shock. That first night we killed a chicken, and it was dreadful, absolutely dreadful. Everyone was near-enough suicidal.

Like many others, Gemma makes the point that the English contingent weren't faring terribly well prior to the arrival of the Americans and Australians. What seems strange, though, is that all but one of the new arrivals were from urban backgrounds, much like the majority of the English themselves. And yet, they somehow seemed to be so much better at roughing it:

Almost all of them were city dwellers, yes, but when I spoke to them, it soon emerged that each of them had done a bit of travelling. Maybe not in the kind of situation we were adapting to then, but they'd certainly done their bit in the past. They'd already spread their wings, whereas a lot of the English people were very city-bound – and it made a huge difference. They were a real blessing. Honestly, if they hadn't come when they did, us guys wouldn't have stood a chance. I'm not joking. In the first place it was a real pick-me-up to see them – different faces, different personalities. But on top of that, they had so much go in them, and they knew what they were talking about.

As we now know, the pick-me-up effect was short-lived for some of the castaways, and Gemma, of course, was one of the members of the 'English girls' group who were shortly to distance themselves from the others. Explaining the reasons behind their decision to do so, she says:

> Well it's hard to explain properly, but when you wake up every day to people shouting orders at you, people talking down to you, it really starts to take its toll. And it wasn't like everyone was addressed on that level – we were really spoken down to, each and every one of us girls. And I agree, sometimes we probably did deserve it – maybe we didn't pull our weight as much as we could have – but we made an effort here and there. Then it got to the point that when we woke up, all the others had already paired off to go and do things, and they'd basically excluded us. We were meant to be a team, so that pissed us off no end.

Naturally enough, if you're not asked to join a team, you form one of your own, which is just what the English girls proceeded to do:

> The day we decided to go off on our own was just *fun*, and it was the first time since arriving that I'd laughed – I'm not exaggerating. It was like being back at primary school, you know, being really naughty and all conniving together. Well, you know what girls are like together. We all got together and planned it out – we all had our secret wolf whistles and secret signals to warn each other if someone was coming. We nicked the pots and the pans, some salt, pepper and oil, then ran down to our little den and hid it all.
>
> Thinking back to it, it might sound a bit childish, but I got such a buzz out of doing something that wouldn't have been a big deal anywhere else. It gave us that extra adrenaline, knowing that we'd been naughty and we were going to get told off. We were laughing and jumping about – it

added excitement to the day, and we really needed that. Just something to make a change from the usual bog-standard average days. Actually it was one of the best days I had out there.

Obviously, the girls' 'fun' was not shared with the rest of the castaways, and yet it was clear from the very start that this was no serious uprising; *Shipwrecked* was *not* about to go all *Lord of the Flies* on us. Even at the time, Gemma kind of knew there'd be slapped wrists, but she had no idea how far the punishment would go. 'The guilt kicked in a few hours later,' she admits. 'Personally, I always looked at it as a game. But when you sit back [and think about it], you realize that what was going on out there *wasn't* a game. I can see why people got so uptight and vexed with us: it wasn't a game, it was real life.'

When that simple bit of fun became the catalyst that eventually led to Genevieve's expulsion, though, the smiles immediately disappeared:

I still can't believe that they took the experience away from someone who'd worked so hard to get there. It killed me. That did me in, and it was so blatantly a case of one rule for one, a different rule for the others. *Everyone* stole something on that island, but only one person got thrown off for it – and if you lay down laws like that, you have to abide by them. I remember when it happened, I was quite surprised by Allan – he'd been so laid-back until then, and I just thought, 'God, Allan, you're being really harsh.' But as the days went by, he was the only one of them that actually showed any remorse. You could see then that it was going to play on his mind.

Talking on the island about the day of Genevieve's departure, Gemma described the event as one of the biggest lows of her time there so far:

> Part of me felt a little jealous that she was going back to the comforts of normal life. When the boat arrived to collect her, my eyes were just filled with tears – I tried so hard to fight them back, but it was too late, I was on an emotional roll by then. So was Gen – she had tears streaming down her face. It was so, so sad… And then all the other members of the group – yes, the ones who'd voted her off – all strolled down to see her off as well! I was so angry then. As soon as she'd gone, the day went on as usual, not even a mention of her name, like she'd never even been there. I was so angry and emotionally drained, I just sat there with Donna and cried my eyes out. The tears just kept coming and coming.

Moreover, Genevieve's expulsion served as the catalyst that set Gemma thinking about leaving too: 'Donna and I started talking about escaping from the island. We keep telling the others that we're staying, and we may yet change our minds, but the way I'm feeling right now, I very much doubt it.'

For every low there would be a high, of course, and just a few days later, Gemma got her groove back in no uncertain terms. Her diary for 22 May starts the theme:

> Boy, do I feel good today. Eyes shining, energy high, spirits alive and positive attitude has kicked in! I walked down to the beach and for the first time, the view really took my breath away. It was absolutely out of this world. The tide was out, the sun was beating down, and the sea was so incredibly calm – and so many beautiful shades of blue.

A smile hit my face and I just thought, 'Gemma, you must be off your head if you want to go back to crappy England and give all this up! You keep saying you miss your life back home, but it'll still be waiting for you when all this is over.'

Four days later, though, Gemma was back down again. 'I feel a little guilty,' she wrote. 'I keep thinking back to the last day I spent with Mum before coming out here. We went shopping and had lunch together and I remember getting a little upset and saying, "Mum, why am I doing this?". So she got all worried and was saying, "Gemma, don't go." Bless her, she always looks out for me.'

Once again, Gemma (along with Donna) started talking about escaping, although it seemed that every option open to them (and there weren't many) was either too dangerous, or was dependent on weather conditions that could not be guaranteed. Eventually, the two girls asked the rest of the cast to vote them off the island on Day 21.

Back in England, Gemma recalls the dilemma clearly:

It's really hard within yourself to come to the decision to leave, really hard to know whether you're doing the right thing. You have to be so sure. There were lots of reasons for leaving – you came to feel like a bit of a pawn: you're putting yourself through all these bad thoughts and emotions, and at the end of the day there's no real reason why you have to do it. I went through a real emotional upset out there, and I didn't think of myself as an especially emotional person before I went. I saw a side to myself a) that scared me, and b) that I certainly didn't like. I felt that I was going to be portrayed totally out of character, totally unhappy, and that's just not me. And when you face that every day, it gets to you. It's like anything – if you wake up every day to a job that you hate, then you've got to change something, do something about it. And I just decided that it wasn't me – I wasn't enjoying it, I wasn't going to gain anything from it, and it would have just done me in if I'd stayed.

The castaways tried to persuade the girls to stick it out, especially Jeffro, who felt that Gemma might only be leaving out of a sense of loyalty to Donna. 'Aw bless him,' she smiles:

Jeffro brought me through some of my darkest moments, he really was a little angel to me. Actually a lot of people thought that I was leaving because of Donna, but I'm not the type to be influenced by people and Donna certainly didn't influence me in the slightest. I'm sure if I could have tapped into that part of my brain that let me forget about all the things I was missing back at home, then yes, I'm sure I could have pulled myself through it. The thing is, I went out there with an expectation. And when you approach anything in life with an expectation and it doesn't meet up to that expectation, it's a disaster. I wish now that I'd gone with no idea [about what it would be like], but I didn't.

The group eventually admitted defeat, and held a vote to nominate the two willing evictees off the island. All but Geordie and Shawn voted for them to go. And in one of the sweetest farewell notes, Malia wrote, 'You make all the boys go weak at the knees when you smile, and I should hate you for that, but Gem, honey, you're one of the most lovely and humble chicks around. You're certainly the only girl I know who can walk around in a G-string without looking like a show-off.'

Looking back on the experience, Gemma has – to say the least – mixed feelings about her time on Yaukuvelevu:

There wasn't a community. Not while we were there, at least. If there'd been more of a team feeling then it might have been a different story, but it just wasn't there. We'd say we were going to work at that, and everyone agreed that it was a good idea and all that, but by the next day it was forgotten and it was a totally different story. Nobody really spoke to each other, nobody really said what they thought, and if they did it was generally after they'd blown up about something, and by then it was too late. You'd be surprised how little conversation there was. And if I'm honest, people got to me after a while. A lot of them were real extroverts. I'm not used to being spoken down to, and certainly not by the likes of Salvo. I mean, I'm a strong person myself, but on the island you had so many different personalities, so many different opinions, you just [gave] up fighting after a while. I don't know... we didn't act like adults, really. I think every person was slightly fake, and because there were cameras about, people were always more concerned about saying something witty or doing something that would catch people's eye. There were people who bugged me, of course there were, but it's like friends in everyday life – they can bug you as well.

She pauses and laughs. 'You know what's really funny?' she giggles. 'I saw the second series of *Shipwrecked*, where that young girl, Vicki, had decided to leave the island, and I'm not kidding, I was jumping off my sofa screaming "You *idiot*!" I was going crazy at the TV, thinking how can that girl be throwing away an opportunity like that? And six months later I was doing exactly the same thing! I suppose the truth is, I'm a quitter – but I had my reasons. So you can put me in the book as "The Weakest Link",' she laughs, 'I really don't mind!'

Of course, having told all her friends and family that she was embarking on this *Shipwrecked* experience, Gemma now had the unenviable task of explaining to them why she'd come home before even reaching the halfway mark:

It's funny. I really haven't spoken to many people about it since I got back – I've blanked it, like it was a figment of my imagination. I haven't wanted to speak about it. Some of my friends were saying 'You *idiot*. Not even a month out there and you've packed it in.' But then when you explain that there was no food, they change their thinking pretty quickly. The truth of the matter is, if it *had* been like the past series, we'd have sailed through it. It's that food factor – it really does do you in. I couldn't afford to lose any more weight – when I came back half the weight on me was the acne on my face! I just felt totally ill. Didn't do me any favours on the health front, I can tell you. If I'm honest, I was unsure about going on the island in the first place, but I was *so* sure about leaving, and I've not regretted it since.

Her family, of course, were just pleased to have her back:

I was *so* happy when I got home. If you ask any of my family they'll tell you that coming home was the best thing I've ever done. Because the state I was in when I got back to England really wasn't nice. Sure, there's a small part of them that was upset, but for the most part they were happy that I'd had the confidence to turn round and say, 'OK, I can't do this.' It was extremely hard for me to do that – you feel that you've let yourself and your family down. And I was really worried what people would say – that they'd think I was a failure and an idiot. But there isn't a single person who has

– each one of them's patted me on the back and said, 'Well done'. I'm sure there'll be people watching it on the TV who think 'Well that's not so bad, I could do that', but they have *no* idea what it's like; it would blow them away.

I know I sound like I'm talking it down, but when I think back to it, every single bit of it was good in its own way. Everything I did taught me something. It's advanced me. I've seen a lot of changes in myself. I appreciate the very smallest of things – you just appreciate how lucky we are. We're so fortunate and we don't even know it. And the people on the island? I've got nothing but the hugest respect for all of those that pulled through and did it. Each and every one of the castaways had a lovely quality about them – for every negative thing you could say about someone, there were ten positive things to outweigh the bad stuff. They all brought something of themselves to the island, and it might not be immediately noticeable, but I can guarantee it was there; just something that made another person's day that little bit better.

4

CHLOE-JANE
EVERTON

Age: 22
Profession: PE teacher
Luxury Item: Football

Chloe-Jane Everton would be the first to admit that she's something of a tomboy. It was the first observation made about her at the selection weekend, and it soon became apparent to all the castaways that she was no wet blanket – all the proof you need being her choice of luxury item, a football. Throughout the book, you'll see references made to 'The English Girls': a collective noun used for Sarah-Jane, Vicki, Donna, Genevieve and Gemma from day one, when that group established itself almost as a separate faction (neatly overlooking the fact that Genevieve, although resident in London, is actually French).

Chloe-Jane was never part of that splinter group. She rapidly established herself very much as 'one of the boys', but, more importantly, also established herself as an individual. By her own admission, she can come across as a bit of a tough nut, not the kind of girl to break down sobbing at every hurdle, although she claims that her biggest weakness is her appetite. 'My stomach is a bottomless pit,' she admitted before setting off, 'and when I'm hungry, I start to shake and get weak. I've always been like that.

That said, I'll eat anything. And as far as killing animals goes, if needs must, it's got to be done. I wouldn't enjoy it, of course, but I wouldn't have a problem with it.'

As a PE teacher at a secondary school, Chloe-Jane already boasted a level of physical fitness that would serve her well over the ten-week stay: an excellent footballer, she teaches everything from aerobics to rugby, describing herself as being 'up for anything'. Lancashire born and bred, Chloe-Jane admits that some people might find her 'gobby' and hard work, but also stresses that she's essentially cool, calm, and collected... up to a point... 'My temper's completely situation-dependent,' she confesses. 'I can be the most relaxed person, but if there's an issue over something that really matters to me, it's best to stand back – I'm a bit like a volcano erupting.'

Chloe-Jane knows that she can come across as headstrong, even (in her own words), 'a bit of a bitch' at times, but stresses that she's essentially a fun-loving type, always up for a laugh. Her last weekend at home before setting off for Yaukuvelevu, for instance, remains a bit of an unknown quantity: 'All my friends threw a farewell party for me, and I got so drunk,' she blushes. 'I honestly have no memory from 10.00pm onwards, but I woke up battered and bruised from falling down the stairs. Oh, and my boyfriend Ian wasn't talking to me either... but that's a whole different story.'

Uncannily, Chloe-Jane already had a bizarre connection with *Shipwrecked*. Purely by chance, she had found herself on the same plane as the *Shipwrecked* second series cast, and even photographed them all with Andi Peters at Heathrow Airport. She's kept the photo ever since, and was determined, on the back of that encounter, to apply. She's also seen every episode of the previous two series and is something of a *Shipwrecked* expert, although she was quick to point out that just watching the show isn't the same thing as being there. 'You only see a very small fraction of what's going on,' she explains. 'Such a small fraction. It's like ten weeks condensed into ten hours. I'm really looking forward to finding out what goes on behind the scenes.'

Chloe-Jane quickly earned her survival stripes at the selection weekend, proving herself to be a more than capable team member, the only one who mastered the high-rope climbing, and, with no prior experience we hasten to add, effortlessly skinning a rabbit. More than that, though, she emerged as a true team player, one with whom everyone got on. 'We made a pact at the selection weekend,' she later revealed, 'that our primary point in going out to the island was to have fun. To have a good time and enjoy it – I do hope that prevails.' She was very pleased by the final line-up of castaways, although even in those early stages, one of the cast had already made his mark on her. 'Salvo's a character and a half,' she laughs. 'Some of the others are a bit unsure how to take him, but I shared a bivouac with him on the weekend, and he's really funny once you get the hang of him. He's totally laid back. But a bit of a Rambo, if we're honest.'

With all these qualities, it comes as little surprise that the other castaways decided to vote Chloe-Jane in as their first leader on the island. Quite a compliment, on the one hand, but a huge responsibility at the same time. The very first page of Chloe-Jane's diary describes Yaukuvelevu as 'our island of heaven and hell', a prophetically accurate description of the place and one that would be proven time and time again over their ten-week stay. And as the first leader, she somehow had to make sense of it all and hold everyone together.

Picture this – the sound of the boat motor ceases and ten troopers scuttle towards the island, fully clothed, clutching their backpacks and luxury items. One by one, we head towards the golden beaches of our new home. This is the *Shipwrecked* team, and when I say 'team', I mean it — that's exactly what we will have to be from now on, because we're not going to make it through any other way. The only thing I know for certain right now, is that this will be no easy ride. Not even for the toughest amongst us.

At this point, the castaways numbered just ten, with the Australians and Americans yet to arrive on the island. The Brits were immediately aware that things were different this time around, and it can only be seen as the highest of compliments when they unanimously selected Chloe-Jane as the most capable among them and elected her as their leader, which she appreciated, as she subsequently revealed in her diary.

'It seems strange to say this, and when you consider it in the grander scheme of things it may appear a little ridiculous, but I have never felt as proud as the day my nine new friends voted me in as leader. That said, this is no easy task in the first week — this is a new way of life in a different country. There's only ten of us, so it's going to be a lot harder to explore the island, and there's so much ground to cover. We spent that first day scouring high and low, checking out the island's natural resources, which we had been previously told would be in abundance. Our first discovery, surprisingly enough, was a statue on a hill...'

Ah yes. The statue, otherwise known as The Goddess. Welcome to another addition to the all-new *Shipwrecked*. Now, while most of the changes mentioned so far have had the effect of making life on the island much, much harder, it's not like the programme makers are completely heartless. While the castaways' day-to-day existence was harsher, they were also able to look forward to some treats, although they had to be earned, rather than just dropped into their laps.

The Goddess was the castaways' lifeline, if you will. A sort of quasi-spiritual 'Get Out Of Jail Free' card, the idea being that in times of genuine need, they could summon her through prayer and offerings, in return for food. To a Western mindset that might sound faintly absurd, but it's very much in keeping with Fijian culture, and since this experience was all about totally immersing the castaways in this corner of the world, it makes perfect sense to adopt the ancient customs. That said, there were some who found the notion more than a little troubling – but we'll get to their objections later on.

The next discovery was made by Donna and Gemma, who stumbled on the vegetable patch. A bittersweet find, as it turned out. As Chloe-Jane explained, 'This was the first glimmer of hope that shone, and we knew there and then that we would not starve. Or so we thought. On closer inspection, though, we decided that there was much work to be done, since not one vegetable was ripe.'

Grim and grimmer? Well, it was starting to look that way, when at last, a real reason to be cheerful emerged. Close to the vegetable patch were two animal enclosures, one containing two pigs, the other, as Chloe described it, 'filled with twenty-five very anxious-looking chickens. And they had every right to look that way, as the future that awaited them was pretty bleak, if we're honest. I decided there and then to distance myself from the animals because I don't want to grow emotionally attached at all – eventually, they will all be killed for food.'

Those first two days on Yaukuvelevu were largely dedicated to building temporary shelters and exploration. Unlike previous *Shipwrecked* ventures, there was no tarpaulin sheeting, and the castaways really did have to construct their living quarters from scratch, using only bamboo for the frames, and interwoven coconut-tree leaves for the roofs. In short, life was looking very hard, and our ten British castaways were not a happy bunch of

Nice island — we'll take it. The castaways settle into their new home.

The group were startled to find a long-lost TV crew lurking on the beach.

⊕

Simon and Leon suspected that Genevieve had been discarding
some unusually large matches on the beach.

Malia would spend whole days sucking the poison out of Salvo's gnat bites.

⊕

Geordie, Shawn and Randy began to realise that no girls would be coming to the party...

The yam broth lacked a certain 'Je ne sais quoi'.

Simon's first attempt at body art was encouraging, in a basic kind of way.

Shawn had found a new way of scaring the sharks away from the shoreline.

⊕

Leon and Malia weren't entirely convinced by their new sunglasses.

Jeffro made sure that his little brother Spencer gained island immortality.

⊕

Salvo and Leon firmly refuted all accusations that they took pleasure in killing animals. No, really.

Simon, with the one that *didn't* get away.

Allan, being terribly hard, was completely
unphased by his shaving rash.

Geordie, like, totally dug the
pig-smoking oven, man.

Malia and Geordie realised that they'd made their
own bed and would now have to lie in it.

⊕

Geordie realised he had wildly
over-estimated the demand for
his 'lucky fish-heads'.

⊕

Rainbow grilling yet more yams...

Gemma and Donna preparing another
sumptuous yam concoction.

⊕

campers at all. Chloe-Jane weathered it like a trooper, admitting to hiding her own true feelings of desperation, if only for the sake of group morale.

The nights were, in theory, a time for rest. In theory, yes, in practice, sleep soon turned out to have its own bittersweet qualities as well. Chloe summed it up perfectly in her diary entry for Day 2:

We tried sleeping in our shelters but soon abandoned them to kip on the beach, when we realized that a colony of ants had made its way into the huts. And these were no normal ants — we're talking the Jonah Lomus of the ant kingdom: the biggest, fastest, hardest buggers ever, and moreover, they bite. Sleeping on the beach, though, was an experience in itself, and one that I will never ever forget. There was a distinct-smelling warm breeze, the sand was lusciously soft, and above it all you could hear the soft lapping of waves against the shore...

About two hours into a deep sleep, I felt something on the back of my leg. I guessed it was just a mosquito, but it had been enough to wake me up. I looked down, and realised that this so-called 'mosquito' was the size of a grown man's fist, with two huge pincers — yes, a crab had taken it upon itself to take a nap on my leg. One swift slap soon solved this, but I couldn't get back to sleep at all. I spent the rest of the night patrolling the beach on my own.

Tired, hungry and demoralized, our trusty leader can't have been looking forward to Day 3 — although as we've already seen, Yaukuvelevu has an uncanny knack of throwing all kinds of surprises your way, some good, some bad. Day 3's surprise would most definitely be considered one of the better ones on offer.

Before we get to that, though, it's particularly relevant to note that the first act of that day was a meeting to discuss the productivity (or lack thereof) of certain members of the group. Chloe-Jane's solution was to pair people off in groups of two who would work together, each coupling consisting of one stronger person and one (as Chloe-Jane so diplomatically put it) 'less able' person.

Accordingly, this system saw Chloe-Jane and Genevieve teaming up to work in the camp, getting a cooking fire started, when suddenly they heard raised voices and knew that something significant was going on. What happened next was described by Chloe-Jane as 'like getting the present you always really wanted on your birthday. Like winning the lottery, in fact.' The prize? Six new castaways had arrived on the island: three Australians and three Americans — four boys, two girls. We'll allow those newcomers to introduce themselves in time, but for now the really important thing was having six extra pairs of hands to help out. As Chloe-Jane confirmed, 'Productivity that afternoon rocketed, and everyone really mucked in.' The other castaways all confirmed that the arrival of the US/Australian team was a massively needed boost for their flagging spirits, almost like 'being rescued'.

The next meeting that Chloe-Jane summoned would be on Day 6. Several issues required discussion, including one that we've avoided mentioning till now, namely the business of going to the toilet. Thankfully, we won't dwell too long on this subject, but a quick look through the castaways' diaries indicates that bowel movements would rapidly become a source of almost obsessive interest. The team were adjusting to a very different diet to that which they were accustomed to, and their insides all reacted differently to the experience. The toilet facility, as such, was affectionately known as the 'long-drop', a sort of pit that all the castaways were required to use. As there was no toilet paper, leaves were used for wiping, and buckets of sea water to 'flush'.

Even at this early stage, it was emerging that not everyone was doing their bit in the flushing department, this mild laziness being symptomatic of a wider problem. As Chloe-Jane explained, 'There just seemed to be a real disregard for everything. Stuff was being mislaid and not looked after.' 'Stuff' refers to the minimal food supplies (pepper, salt and oil), various tools (machete knifes and so forth), pots, pans, matches and bodycare products (essential sun-protection)... Clearly, this stemmed from a certain lack of organi-sation, although Chloe-Jane was quick to remedy the matter by allocating responsibility for each given area to one of the team. This would be Chloe-Jane's last act as leader, the first week being more or less over. All present were quick to agree that she'd done a superb job, moreover, and would be a hard act to follow.

The next pivotal event in Chloe-Jane's island experience surprised everyone. You've already read, last chapter, about Genevieve's expulsion from Yaukuvelevu for theft, and how that event set a moral precedent for the whole team. As one of those who voted for Genevieve to leave the island, Chloe-Jane was brutally frank, both about the event itself, and – just as importantly – about the fact that any issue of morality could not really be viewed in terms of black and white. 'Everyone said they voted Gen off for stealing, when in actual fact there wasn't one person on that island who didn't steal something at one stage or another,' she freely admitted on returning to England. 'And it's absolutely true, there's no denying that. The reason put forward for expul-sion, then, was stealing, but for me it was more than that – it was a general feeling that it wasn't "All for one and one for all", it was, "All for Genevieve and none for the rest". I'm just as guilty as anyone else, because I took some hot chocolate from Sarah in one of the first few days, but I still don't regret my decision.'

The morality of stealing, then, was a grey area to most. But much further on in the stay, Chloe-Jane would – along with Malia

– make the conscious decision to deprive the islanders of one particular source of nutrition that would make a couple of spoons of drinking chocolate seem trivial.

It all started on Day 19, 27 May – Jeffro's birthday. A momentous event in itself (like all of the Yaukuvelevu birthdays), and one that saw two goats being added to the castaways' livestock resources. One of the goats was later confiscated, leaving just one, called Thomas. And it was Thomas that Chloe-Jane and Malia decided to liberate, without consulting any of the others. Not to steal it, as such – it's not like they planned on eating it – merely to set it free, to spare its life. The plan involved constructing a small raft, one that could be used to ferry the goat to safety, a plan that was almost thwarted when the raft was discovered.

As Chloe-Jane wrote in her diary, on Day 53:

> I *love* mischief. Everyone here thinks they know everything, and that just makes me giggle. Tonight Randy announced that he'd found a small raft. He assumed that Malia had made it, and before long, everyone was working on the theory that Malia was planning to escape from the island – no one suspected me at all. Randy and Leon asked me if I knew anything, but I just played dumb.

The discovery of the raft, however, meant that the plan had to be executed as soon as possible. Just two days later, in fact. Now, at low tide, it would be possible to return the goat to the island it originally came from, the two girls carrying it on the raft between them. As Chloe-Jane admitted in her diary:

> It was actually really exciting, and I was quite nervous about being caught. I woke Malia and she went down to fetch the goat right away. I really didn't want to fail, because if we

were intercepted there was the risk that the others might try to kill Thomas. In truth, I hadn't been happy with the treatment of some of the animals we'd already killed — there'd been a certain lack of respect shown. Salvo in particular disrespected animals after killing them — he'd slap the carcass around, and various bits of their anatomy as a pretend mobile phone for the sake of a joke.

It's worth noting that Chloe-Jane, in common with all the castaways, had mixed feelings about Salvo. Back in England she summed it up thus, 'He's the most unique person I have ever come across in my life and no doubt I will never meet anyone like him again. He is one crazy person. One minute you'd be in hysterics with him, and the next you'd be pulling out your hair and screaming at him because he could be so impossible.' This love/hate relationship is one that would emerge again and again in the course of the ten weeks, but for now, Chloe-Jane felt that the fate that awaited Thomas was a less than dignified one, and that this was reason enough to set him free. 'I knew I was doing the right thing,' she maintains, 'although whether everyone else would see it the same way, I wasn't so sure.'

As it was, the two girls were spotted carrying Thomas away from the island by Randy, Salvo and Leon who — much to Chloe-Jane's surprise — all stood and cheered their actions. The liberation effort was successful: Thomas bounded off to a far rosier future on a neighbouring island, and the girls returned to face the music. Chloe-Jane, for her part, was defiant about the whole episode. 'I was so relieved,' she wrote. 'I felt like a hero, and [felt] that justice had been done. I didn't care abut facing the others when I got back, and I didn't honestly care about the consequences of my actions.'

On reaching Yaukuvelevu, the two-woman animal liberation front immediately called a meeting to explain what they'd done.

As Chloe-Jane stressed, there had never been any question of her and Malia attempting to conceal the matter, and they were more than happy to accept the group's judgement. The group's response, was, they were relieved to find, almost universally OK. With one distinct exception, namely Allan. We'll come to that in his chapter, but for now, let's just say that he was partly troubled by the moral implications and partly suspicious of Chloe-Jane's motives in liberating Thomas. As Chloe-Jane wrote in her diary, though, 'It would only take a small chat with my friends and family for anyone to realize my passion for animals. I would argue that sometimes you have to be cruel to be kind, and I was perhaps cruel to the group in being kind to the goat. Yes, we had less in terms of food, but what it stood for meant so much more.'

Chloe-Jane, as all her fellow castaways would immediately confirm, proved herself to be a born survivor, and – without wishing to sound too grand about it – an inspiration to the people around her. Back on home turf, she maintains that despite the occasional lows of the experience, there's not a single moment that she regrets.

'It was tremendously harsh, and everyone felt it,' she confirms. 'There's not a single person there who didn't complain at one point in the day. We were incredibly hungry, no one would deny that. But it changed on a day-to-day basis – some days you'd wake up in the best of moods, you'd be lying next to someone and smiling no matter how hungry you were, just because it was so fantastic to be there. Then the next day, it'd be raining, and everyone would be miserable for forty-eight hours, and it would be just the lowest low in the world.'

Ask her if she ever contemplated throwing in the towel and leaving the island, and she immediately responds, 'Loads of times, and I think anyone who said any different would be telling porky-pies. I saw even the strongest of characters going through those periods. We'd have little chats with each other to try and pull through it, but all of us at some point or another felt like throwing the towel in. You'd be telling yourself it's not reality, it's just a telly programme. Then again, there were days when you were so up, where there wasn't anything that anyone could do to you that would make you want to leave.

'I've thought about it long and hard since I got back to England,' she continues, 'and I can honestly say that there's nothing I regretted doing or not doing while I was out there. It's funny – you think about it all so much, and it's absolutely incredible how much stuff goes through your mind, the number of ridiculous scenarios that come up in your head. But there's honestly not a single moment that I regret.' She goes quiet for a moment then breaks into a huge smile. 'You know what? I actually really miss it all. I've really missed being there – I think I could actually 'live' there. Perhaps not in exactly the same circumstances... I'd certainly want to choose who I went with. But there are days back in England when I'd much rather be out there digging up some yams for dinner. Much as we moaned about the food out there, it was absolutely brilliant.'

And Chloe-Jane would be the first to agree that you don't go through this kind of experience without something rubbing off on you, without it changing you, in however small a way. 'I'm definitely a more reasonable person now,' she smiles.

I don't always take things on face value either – I'm very willing to listen to the other side of the story these days. The thing that I've noticed more than anything is that I want to share what I've got. My boyfriend's noticed it on several occasions – the fact that I want to hand-feed him from my plate. If we go to a restaurant for a meal, before I've even had a bite of my own food I'll cut a bit off for him to try and shove it in his mouth. I do it with my family as well, and it's really bizarre.

I'm cooking a lot as well, trying all sorts of recipes. You missed food so much out there, I can't begin to tell you – I never thought I'd find myself in a situation where food governed ninety per cent of your thought processes. If you weren't talking about the food you missed, you were talking about the food you were going to eat when you got back.

She freely admits to one small pang of envy, though.

I'm really jealous I didn't have a birthday on the island to be honest with you. Birthdays were so important out there. It wasn't really just one person's birthday that we were cele-brating – it became 'everyone's' birthday. It gave you some-thing to do, something to talk about. You'd be making a pres-ent for someone else, but it made you just as happy to be making it [as it would to receive it]. Birthdays were some-thing that everyone could join in with and everyone could celebrate. I actually had my birthday shortly after getting back to England, and I told people I didn't want them to get me anything unless it was something they'd made them-selves. That's the theme of my birthday... handmade goods.

For Survival School, then, it would only be fair to award Chloe-Jane Everton ten out of ten. Without being immodest, she professes herself to have always had every confidence that she would see it through. 'I think deep down I always knew I was capa-ble – I can be a very stubborn, hard-faced person who won't let anything defeat me. At the same time,' she adds, 'I don't think any one of us could have done it without the others. It wasn't so much about "me" surviving as "all of us" surviving.

5

JEFF
BRAZIER

aka 'Jeffro'
aka 'J-to-the-E-to-the-double-F-RO'

Age: 21 on arrival, 22 when he left the island
Profession: Footballer (semi-professional)
Luxury Item: A souvenir photo album of his
   pre-*Shipwrecked* farewell party, containing
   messages from all his friends and family.

That luxury item (Jeffro himself describes it as 'a bit of a girly item') speaks volumes about the man you're about to meet. For Jeffro, it's always been about family: not just the family you're born into, but the one you create for yourself as well, ie the friends you surround yourself with. And if this were an American talk show, you'd have some balding bloke with a moustache lecturing you about the importance of 'nurturing' that family, about never taking it for granted. Mercifully, it's not. Besides which, Jeffro puts it so much better himself. 'I just feel responsible for the group around me for some reason,' he admits. 'If everyone else is happy, then I'm happy. And I do what-ever it takes to keep it that way.'

Even on the selection weekend, that much became clear, as Jeffro recalled before setting off to the island:

What was really nice about that weekend was that there was no one trying to be above anyone else. I always say 'Help everyone to help yourself.' You know, when you're doing team games, don't try to be the star, because when you succeed as a team you feel better for yourself. And when you think about it, there were so many applicants, so each of the ones who got through must have something about them, something special. Great people. You really get the feeling that you've made friends for life. I can't wait to see everyone again.

That selection weekend was so much fun. Best weekend ever, but also the worst in some ways – I know it sounds like a cliché, but it really was an emotional rollercoaster: you're so happy you've gotten through, and then you look at the people who didn't make it and think, 'Hang on, I really liked them, I really wanted to spend some time with them.' It was very up and down, but it was amazing how quickly you bonded with people. Even Salvo! I mean, he's completely bananas, is Salvo, and at the weekend he was the only person I felt was giving me dirty looks – I guess he felt a bit of an outsider because of the language barrier. But I'm glad I made the effort with him.

Jeffro admitted to being concerned in advance about how the viewers would perceive him, but was characteristically philosophical about it: 'I think the viewers might not know what to make of me. I don't think anyone can really give me a label – I'm a bit of everything, you know what I mean? I don't have any plan as such – you know, as soon as you start thinking, "Oh, I'll try and be this way", it immediately comes across as being false. Having an agenda is the last thing you want, 'cos people will see right through it.'

Like many of the other castaways, Jeffro admitted right from the start that part of the appeal of *Shipwrecked* was the fact that he'd be on national television. That said, this wasn't a simple 'Look at me!' exercise for Mr Brazier, it was less about being famous, more about what it would mean to the people who would be watching him: 'My friends and family are already so proud of me, even though I haven't done that much so far – just got selected. I'll tell you what, though, I can't wait for my little brother Spencer to sit down and see his big brother on the telly.'

Jeffro's concern for Spencer comes up time and time again in conversation. Ask him what makes him angry and he immediately replies, 'Other people's cruelty. Spencer has cerebral palsy, and the comments he gets from other children, and even from adults, are so harsh. I can't begin to explain the frustration he must feel, and I really wish people would educate their children better. But then, that's the way of the world, and if anything, Spencer is a stronger little man because of it.'

Jeffro decided, then, that Spencer would, in his own little way, become part of the *Shipwrecked* experience. On arrival at Yaukuvelevu, the castaways soon discovered a boat that had been provided for them. With the unanimous approval of the group, Jeffro named the boat *HMS Spencer*, and immediately set about carving out a nameplate to attach to it.

And in a wholly unplanned and sweetly poetic turn of events, *HMS Spencer* would make her maiden voyage on Jeffro's twenty-second birthday, 27 May, otherwise known as 'Day 19'. 'In all honesty, I was worried that because of the distance between me, friends and family, that the day would turn out to be a non-event,' he admits, 'but on the other hand, I sort of believed that people would do their best to make it as nice a day as possible. But I'll be honest, I was completely unprepared for all the surprises and effort that people made for me, and for that I'll be eternally grateful.'

The day started early, and abruptly, as all the other castaways silently crept up to surround Jeffro, who was still sleeping soundly in his hammock. He woke to a raucously rousing chorus of 'Happy Birthday To You', before being held aloft by his fellow shipwreck-ees and carried down to the beach, where he was unceremoni-ously dumped into the water. Leon then dived in to deliver an Aussie birthday tradition, a punch on the arm for every year. Allan's characteristically wry observation was to label it, 'not an Aussie best. It probably seems hilarious when you're drunk, but I think we stop doing that on about the fourteenth birthday in England.' Of course, it didn't trouble Jeffro, who conceded, 'Oh well, at least it helped me wake up.'

The next stage of the celebrations was the official naming ceremony for *HMS Spencer*: everyone watched as Jeffro attached his handmade sign to the boat, before asking Rainbow to say a few words. In the absence of champagne, a plastic bottle was 'smashed' against the boat's prow. It was, as Jeffro would later admit, 'a real lump-in-the-throat moment.'

You can't have a birthday without presents, of course, and Jeffro had a sneaking suspicion that a visit to The Goddess was in order, just on the off-chance that something might have been provided for the big day, although he joked that the birthday surprise would probably turn out to be a custard pie in his face. He was wrong about the pie, of course, but just as surprised by what he *did* find, namely a treasure map, a large 'X' marking the spot they had to find. The snag? The X was actually on another island, one lying two miles away. *HMS Spencer* was about to take to the Fijian seas.

It remained only to select a crew of five to go on the journey, the team (after a certain amount of faffing and bickering) being

Salvo, Geordie, Malia, Leon and of course the Birthday Boy himself. 'It was so exciting!' recalls Jeffro. 'We all set off and it only took us an hour to reach the other island, where we quickly found the location marked on the map. And there they were, my birthday presents, and they were *great*. Two goats, two pineapples, a jar of thirty sweets and a litre of cooking oil. Strange choice, but somehow very satisfying.'

On return to the island, the preparations got underway for the first island birthday party, starting with more presents. As Chloe-Jane has already explained, it wasn't a simple matter of choosing something out of an Argos catalogue – you did what you could with what was to hand, but it meant that more so than usually, the thought really did count. Shell necklaces and bracelets, a roll of toilet paper, a handmade chair, all these things might seem less than obvious presents to us, but for Jeffro were the richest gifts he'd ever received. 'It was the best day,' he beams.

I saw the very best in every person on the island. And the dinner! Simon and Rainbow had cooked four chickens, and loads of fried yam – the best meal of my life! Then Chloe-Jane gave it the finishing touch. She'd smuggled some cider-vinegar onto the island, and it just added that bit of flavour, made it one bit better. I had surprises, an adventure, received some very special gifts that I will keep forever, but also I just loved the way it brought everyone together. We were all enjoying ourselves, laughing and joking. I'm just happy that everyone else enjoyed my birthday as much as me, and it just reminded me how close I'm going to be to all of them when we leave the island.

There were, of course, some people who Jeffro got closer to than others, and it's here that one of the great mysteries of the whole series needs to be addressed, namely the apparent lack of romance. Yaukuvelevu was, as all the castaways insisted, a nookie-free zone. The theories behind that are varied, but most of the castaways put it down to the fact that they were largely too tired to contemplate that side of things, and certainly far too busy with the more important matter of day-to-day survival to let anything like that trouble them.

Back at the selection weekend, though, some definite sparks of chemistry had been noticed flashing between Gemma and Jeffro. Immediately after that weekend, Gemma admitted she'd been aware of this: 'I got home and said to my friends, "I think one of the reasons I was picked was because they think a romance is going to blossom." What a lovely guy, though. Jeffro's like the characters I spend time with when I'm home and it felt like I already knew him. He's everybody's friend – he really spreads his energy, rather than channelling it into just the one area. But as for romance, I don't know. I really don't know about that...'

Jeffro, for his part, confessed to being smitten. 'Gemma's smile just tells a million stories. Me and her clicked immediately. As far as romance goes, well, I think it could happen. I know it could, in fact – she's just the right person for me. But at the same time, I wouldn't want to jeopardize a beautiful friendship. Sorry to be boring!'

Jeffro's views on love are a contradictory, if fairly recognizable, blend of optimism and pessimism. 'I thought I loved my ex-girlfriend, Danielle,' he says, 'But I got let down there, and I don't plan on getting close to anyone again, unless they are *extremely* special. If they don't have that, I'd rather not bother – I'd rather be free and single and enjoy my younger years, to be honest.'

Once bitten, twice shy, then. But while we're certainly not about to suggest that Jeffro's some kind of Casanova, there was also talk, if only briefly, about the possibility of something developing between him and Sarah-Jane. That particular relationship would also remain platonic, as it turned out, later growing into one of the most genuinely touching and affirming friendships to be born out of the ten-week stay.

As Jeffro admits, though, there was an ambiguity there for a while:

At first there was, you know, possibly something that was going to develop there between us. When we did our training just before heading out to the island, we were on these bunks, and all of a sudden I woke up at four in the morning, and Sarah-Jane was getting a bit fresh, if you know what I mean... It went a *little* way, and then it just stopped in its tracks. I mean there were eight other people in the room! But after that, I just said to her, look, I really, really think the world of you, but I don't think it's going to do either of us any good if we get into anything like that. And I genuinely believed that — it wasn't just some kind of knock-back. I mean, Sarah-Jane's really beautiful, and people couldn't understand why nothing went on, no sex or anything, but the fact was we just grew so close.

If you see a pattern emerging here, then the *third* name to be romantically linked to Jeffro might well come as a surprise. It started with a few rumours flying about the camp, the day after Vicki's birthday. You'll recall that this was probably the wildest night on the island, certainly in terms of alcohol consumption, although there was a payback to come in the groggy form of The Morning After. While castaways were picking themselves up off the floor, and piecing together the events of the previous night, it was claimed that during a sequence of extremely merry visits to HutCam, Jeffro and Randy had enjoyed a brief, drunken snog.

'Don't you *dare* let that go anywhere near the book!' laughs Jeffro. 'The thing is, Randy gets so drunk that he forgets what's happened the night before. And we were *really* drunk that night, going into the HutCam, doing all kinds of stupid stuff – in the morning, someone decided to wind Randy up and said, "Did you know you snogged Jeff last night?" And he believed it! I soon put him straight on that, if you'll excuse the pun.' Significantly, perhaps, there's no mention of any of this in Randy's diary...

It's probably fair to say, then, that Jeffro is as close as we'll get to a 'Yaukuvelevu Stud', but that's only the tiniest part of the reputation he carried away with him. The bigger picture reveals a guy who was arguably the biggest boost to island morale, one who took it upon himself to see others through their low moments, whilst keeping his own to himself. Now, it's always a bit of a worry when people seem to spend all their time looking after others, leaving no time to reflect on their own issues, but as Jeffro insists, 'Dealing with other people's problems is a good way of taking your mind off your own.' He'd be the first to admit he had his lows (at the end of the first week, he remarked 'Surely prison would be an easier ride than this?'), but found his own way of coping, namely to write a letter to himself. And he gave himself the hardest time, as well.

'Are you being an idiot or what!?' he wrote, on one of the rain-stops-play days:

The weather will get better, the food isn't *that* bad, you're only working for a couple of hours a day! Are you mental? That's what everyone dreams of, and you have the cheek to moan? You're on a tropical island with some great people who are all special in their own right, and because of a bit of bad weather you get all down in the dumps. You're not as mature and well-educated in the ways of the world as you think you are, Jeffro! There. Not a bad bit of writing,

Jeff-boy – you've told yourself off for being an idiot, and you already feel better for it.

Accentuating the positive worked as well on others as on himself; again, it was all part of that, 'If everyone else is happy, then I'm happy' ethic. 'If there was something wrong, if someone was upset, I tried to help them,' he explained, on returning to England. 'But I got the impression that some people didn't care that much how they made other people feel, so long as they were getting by OK. Which is kinda selfish, but in a situation like that you can't expect everyone to be mature enough to cope with it.'

'I know it was tough,' he continues, 'but if we just stopped moaning about the petty stuff, the stupid things... That was one thing I was proud of – I went out there determined not to get involved in that, bitching about people and all that. And I think I managed it – I didn't get involved in the playground stuff. I had a few arguments, mainly with Salvo. Basically because he was antagonizing people. He's a twenty-three-year-old man, but in many ways he's a twelve-year-old. I had a fair few arguments with him, I have to say – he used to make Sarah-Jane cry, and he pretty much made Donna leave. He had a go at her because she did something that he didn't like, something that took attention away from him, and you're not allowed to do that with Salvo. If you do, he reacts like a kid. Not on our island, you know what I mean? We make the rules. In the end, we just pretty much let him get on with it, because you know what? We just couldn't be bothered with him crying and moaning – it was just pathetic and everyone hated it. He can stay in Sicily, that one,' he chuckles, 'go and do some striptease or something.'

Safe to say that those two probably won't be exchanging Christmas cards, then, but Salvo was probably the only one who managed to upset Jeffro in any way. And the others?

The people who lasted till the end, well you just looked around and thought, bloody hell, I don't know how we got through this. Seven people jumped ship – it was really, really tough. I was so naïve – I thought I was going to go out there and have some fun on a beach like the kids in the last series. But when I got there, well, it was disappointing, it was chal-lenging, disappointing, exciting... you went through so many emotions out there, and the thing is they were so intense – everything became really important. You're in such a small environment with so many larger-than-life characters who you're bound to clash with. Everybody really had to look at themselves. I know I did.

In that hyper-sensitive community, Jeffro quickly established himself as a good thing in a bad world, and remains particularly pleased at the role he played in Sarah-Jane's progress over the ten weeks. 'I'm so proud of what I did for Sarah-Jane,' he beams. 'I really clicked with her, like a sort of brother and sister thing.' Ask him to pinpoint the root of her problem and he immediately responds, 'Food. It was the be-all and end-all in every argument out there, but Sarah-Jane, whenever she was cooking something, she'd sit there with Vicki, eating it while she was cooking. She was terrible! I told her so, as well, I said "You really bring it on your-self, you really do." But honestly, she grew so much as the weeks went by. All she wanted was to be respected. All she had to learn was how to earn it. So I told her, and the transition was immedi-ate. I just encouraged her each time she did something. It's basic psychology, isn't it? If someone's afraid of doing something, you just gently push them towards doing it.'

Where he succeeded with Sarah-Jane, however, Jeffro still feels he failed with Gemma. 'I thought that I'd cracked Gemma,' he frowns:

After that Genevieve business, I really tried to get her to stay. I know we were meant to be the couple of the island, and all that, but I didn't really see that in her, not that kind of attraction. But I did see something in her, felt something really deep for her. She's a great person – just had a beautiful way about her. And the reason she went was part of that – she'd really taken Donna under her wing. Basically, Donna was having a really tough time, while I reckon that Gemma could have hacked it – she would have made the whole ten weeks... it's like they say, when you're around positive people, you're gonna feel good and think positive. But Donna was continually thinking about going home, she just didn't want to be there. And when you're around that, it's bound to rub off.

At times it's hard to get Jeffro to talk about himself (he's so busy talking about other people) but he certainly feels he came out of the experience a wiser and better man:

I know it came as a shock when we arrived on the island, but I'm really grateful looking back that it was so tough – you come out a better person for it. It's really hard to explain what it was like without going on and on at someone for ages. A lot of what happened out there will only ever be really understood by the people who were on the island. I never thought seriously about going home – I knew one hundred per cent that I was staying. Perhaps because I felt responsible, you know, because I wanted to be there for other people. I also felt I didn't want to let anyone down at home, and deep down, I just knew I could make it.

Jeffro admitted to worrying what the other shipwreckees would say about him on their return, but needlessly so. His fellow cast-aways shared the unanimous view that Jeffro was a good sort, a man with a heart the size of a planet, and a character who made the whole experience much more fun than it might otherwise have been. All of them spoke of him with some level of affection, but it was an off-the-cuff observation by Chloe-Jane that probably best described Jeffro's charm: 'The guy even smiles in his sleep. 'That just sums him up, really.'

6

ALLAN
BRIDGES

Age: 25
Profession: Charity worker
Luxury Item: A windball ('halfway
between a tennis ball and a football')

Whereas many of the castaways had spoken confidently of their chances of being selected, there was one who – even halfway through the ten weeks on the island – still remained a little unsure as to why he'd been chosen. 'I'd seen the first two series on the telly,' explains Allan, 'and I knew that I wasn't really like the kind of people they usually choose. On top of that, my video didn't come out quite as planned, so I wasn't sure if it was a wind-up when I got the call inviting me along to the selection weekend.'

Once at the weekend, a quick look around at all the other applicants did little to reassure him. 'I immediately saw forty-nine people who *were* like the usual *Shipwrecked* people,' he laughs, 'so I thought my chances were pretty slim. But on reflection, maybe it was a good thing that I was different. The way I had it figured, they were looking for certain types of people, so that left me fighting for the "normal bloke" place. You know, I'm not particularly tall, not particularly gifted, so there's nothing particularly outstanding about me. But I was quite laid-back and funny, I suppose. I think that's why they picked me: to be laid-back, funny and lazy. So it wasn't as though I was going to have to act too hard.'

He actually wasn't far wrong in his assessment. Allan was largely selected because he was naturally witty, his observations at the selection weekend proving him to be an astute commentator, his calmness providing a refreshing, and arguably vital antidote to some of the 'ME, ME, ME!' contingent. 'Oh, there were plenty of people acting up for the camera,' he confirmed, 'elbowing their way to the front of the group and suddenly throwing orders about.' Smiling mischievously, he added, 'I'm twenty-five − I'm not about to be bossed about by an eighteen year-old who hasn't got a clue what they're doing, and only wants to be famous.'

When that comment came back to haunt him after the *Shipwrecked* experience, he was quick to point out that it had been made with tongue firmly in cheek (much of what we hear coming out of Allan's mouth carries a similar disclaimer), but was also quick to point out that 'age became completely irrelevant on Yaukuvelevu, to be honest. Geordie's the oldest twenty-one-year-old I've ever met, and Randy was one of the youngest blokes there, and I got on just as well with him as with any of the others. Probably a lot better, in fact.'

As far as the TV-exposure issue went, Allan was philosophical:

I think once we got out there, the TV thing mattered for some people more than others, but it wasn't like you didn't have any choice − it's not like *Big Brother*, it's not like you had cameras on you every second of the day. If you wanted to get away, you could − for whole days at a time if you really wanted. And also you get quite friendly with the crew while they're with you − it's like having a few extra faces about, [it's] just [that] one of them's got a box on his shoulder. On a day-to-day basis, the cameras didn't make much difference to what we did at all. You go to dig yams because you need to eat, not because you think it'll make you look glamorous on television.

Apart from his age, there was another difference between Allan and the rest of the castaways that would come up time and time again in the seven (yes, *seven*) diaries that Allan kept whilst on the island. Let's just say that if you're thinking it's only women who ask 'Does my bum look big in this?', you couldn't be more wrong. After learning he'd been selected, Allan started going to the gym, managing to lose a stone before he set off for the South Pacific, but even then, his diaries were littered with self-deprecating comments about his weight, and constant reminders to himself that the camera adds a certain number of pounds to a person's appearance. (The figure generally quoted is ten pounds, but in Allan's mind this had been rounded up to a full stone.)

Put it to him that he possibly worried a lot more about this subject than anyone else did, and he shrugs: 'I'll tell you why I talked about it so much – I just know that if I saw a bloke who looked like me on *Shipwrecked*, I'd be ripping it out of him. Let's face it, I'm not the sort of person you're expecting to see. You've got all these young people, and then there's this slightly larger guy, with slightly less hair... You've got Randy and Jeffro, who were the keen sports players, all chiselled muscles and six-packs, so yes, I was quite conscious of the fact that I looked a bit different.'

As for the wealth of written material that Allan took away from the island, well, he was quick to admit that he was never going to be one of the island supermen. Not that he was lazy, as such, but with faultless logic he soon worked out that there were certain castaways who positively enjoyed doing the action man jobs, all the more so when there was a camera present, and if they were happy to deal with the hard stuff, who has he to stop them? 'We were given survival training before going out to Yaukuvelevu,' he explains, 'you know, how to build a hut, how to climb a coconut tree, but I didn't pay the blindest bit of attention, really, just hoped that someone else would be listening because I wasn't that interested. Then you get to the island itself and you realize that you're not actually going to get anything – there's just a cleared-out area; no huts or anything, just some basic provisions.'

Allan was quick to point out, however, that it wasn't as though anyone had been misled regarding the new regime. People had gone on the trip with their own assumptions and expectations based on previous series, and despite being told to expect something very different, they'd still clung to those preconceptions.

We were warned that it was going to be harder, but you never really believe that. We were told that it wasn't going to be a walk in the park, but you sort of assume they're just trying to scare you a bit. The first real dawning of how hard it was going to be came on the third day when we still hadn't eaten anything, because we couldn't catch anything. Us English people were so useless at everything – we just didn't have a clue. We could build huts, but that was about it. At the same time, you kept reminding yourself that it was never going to reach a stage where you would actually starve – it's not like the programme makers were going to stand by and let us suffer from malnutrition.

And let's face it, for a man who'd voiced concerns about his weight, there was an upside to being deprived of food, and the effects were soon noticed by the others. 'Towards the end of the first week I was just wandering about the campsite with no shirt on,' recalls Allan, 'and Salvo suddenly pipes up, "Hey Allan, mate – you're really losing weight." I was pleased he'd noticed. Then he added, "Another two or three years on this island and you might look OK! You were really fat!" I just thought, "OK, Salvo, cheers – that's enough." Those words could really hurt me,' he laughed, 'scar me for life.'

While Allan was quick to make a joke of any given situation, there were some matters that he took as seriously as the rest of the castaways – in some cases, more so. The need to adapt beliefs and behaviour to this unknown environment was, in his mind, one of the keys to surviving the experience, and the heightened emotional state of all the castaways was something he'd picked up on in the very early stages. 'It was like every single action or word was magnified a thousand times,' he recalls, 'and I noticed that right on the first day. Some of us set about building huts, but some of the others just lay on the beach sunbathing, and those of us who were building were absolutely fuming, absolutely furious. Immediately you realize that everything out there is going to be a lot more serious than it would normally be, a lot more important.'

The importance of a group ethic was one that Allan adhered to throughout, and ultimately to his own cost, but perhaps surprisingly, he admits that it's not his usual approach back at home. 'Back in England I'm a "greed is good" capitalist,' he reveals in his diaries. 'Take what you can, get ahead for yourself and by yourself. On Yaukuvelevu, it's like a totally different Allan, a whole new beast.' Perhaps instrumental in bringing about that transformation was the start of the rumours concerning Genevieve's alleged pilfering, combined with Chloe-Jane's observation that the group's provisions were being treated too casually. If the group wasn't automatically making the effort to maintain some level of order, it was clear that people would have to be allocated individual responsibilities. For Allan, this would mean the birth of Al's Shop, a store where the provisions were to be kept and – once borrowed – returned on pain of, er, well not *death*, obviously, but certainly open to receive one of Allan's biting put-downs in the privacy of his diary pages.

Allan embraced the need to change, if seeming a little under-whelmed at the distinct lack of glamour offered by his new role:

> At home I hate the socialist/communist ideal. You know, an extended family where individuals work hard for the bene-fit of the whole group. But here, it's the only system that works. You have to share everything equally. It needs trust and respect, and until such time as that happens automati-cally, it looks like I'll have to look after stuff and dish it out. I've become the quartermaster, a job I fell into. The reluc-tant shopkeeper.

But if Allan moaned about it, he did so – as per usual – in good humour and took it all with a hefty pinch of salt. Later on, he'd describe his position in the group as, 'Lower than Ian Beale. At least he had more than just the one store! This isn't right – I'm sitting here, and I'm actually envious of the saddest television character known to man – Ian sodding Beale.'

It was Allan who observed and documented so many of the little day-to-day aspects of Yaukuvelevu life. Whereas others would wax lyrical about the derring-do of animal slaughter and ration runs, he managed to find time to comment on the more mundane aspects of living on the island, but also managed to make it inter-esting. Whole pages of his diary were devoted to the fact that he went the first six days without a bowel movement, including some unrepeatably detailed description of what it was like when he finally *did* manage to go. 'Well, when they're not happening, they become quite important,' he would later explain. But that's the beauty of his attention to detail: you don't just get the events, you get the sounds and smells that flesh those happenings out.

By way of an example, the castaways' habit of communal sleeping may sound very sweet and idyllic, but there was another side to it as well, as Allan revealed in his diary:

Now, I'm not a nasty person by any stretch of the imagination, and probably the worst accusation that can be levelled at me is that I write the truth at certain times. This is one of those times: Malia smells. She hasn't been near the sea in ages and is now suffering the effects. Or rather, *I'm* suffering the effects. It was so bad last night that I had to spend the entire night facing away from her in a continual search for fresh, breathable air. I can't bring myself to mention it to her though, so I guess you can add 'cowardice' to my list of faults.

It was on Day 30 that others started adding their own contributions to that list, as that day marked the start of Allan's first week as leader. The response was, it's fair to say, mixed. In his diary, he wrote about how much he hated meetings, but noted the positive side of being leader: 'I chair the meetings and control them as well. People won't murmur, or they'll be asked to leave, they won't shout or they'll be asked to leave, each on a three-strikes-then-out basis. I made it crystal clear that I wasn't going to take any crap in meetings, and there was none. Oh, well, I had to shut Salvo up a couple of times, but that's only to be expected. After all, he is a nut.'

The others' reaction to this no-nonsense style was less enthusiastic. Geordie, on the one hand, was critical of Allan's refusal to dish out orders, while Randy, on the other hand, was positively unimpressed by the next meeting, when Allan announced that the castaways' habit of using slightly dampened tampons as toilet paper would have to stop there and then. As Randy wrote in his diary:

I like Allan a lot, but this leader thing seems to be going to his head a little. He actually said that if anyone was caught stealing tampons they would be put to a vote for expulsion from the island, since that was the same reason we voted Genevieve off the island. I mean, come on!!! Stealing? He's got to be kidding! Most of the girls here don't even have periods, because they've been doubling up on birth-control pills. The way I see it, I'm using tampons that Genevieve, Donna or Gemma would have used before they left.

Now, the mention of Genevieve's eviction is key here. While Allan was one of the three who made the nomination for her eviction and one of the eight who voted for her to go, it was never an act that he relished. And from the day she left the island, there was a sense that a very firm precedent had been set, and that the castaways themselves were honour-bound to live by the rules that they'd imposed on Genevieve. To do otherwise, would have been to expose themselves as hypocrites, and — ultimately — to admit that they'd stolen something far bigger from her than anything she ever stood accused of stealing from them.

This insistence on absolute fairness would play heavily in Allan's reaction to Chloe-Jane and Malia's decision to liberate one of the goats, as he recalled back in England:

The group was quite tense that day. Something was going on in secret, which was making everyone uneasy. We actually thought Chloe-Jane and Malia were trying to escape, so when they called a meeting, I thought it was to announce they were leaving, and I didn't bother going. I just thought, 'If you want to go, then go, I've got no interest in it.' I came back about half an hour later and they told me what had happened. And I couldn't get it out of my head that it was stealing. It wasn't their goat, it was the group's goat. We'd been saving it for 4 July, saving it for a good reason. I just couldn't get my head round the fact that they'd taken a decision like that on their own. I was furious with them, to be honest.

At this late stage in the island experience, one particular expression was being bandied about by anyone who needed to rationalize an action that they either didn't understand or didn't approve of – namely, '(s)he's only doing it for television exposure.' Now, it needs to be stressed that that was very rarely the truth of the matter, but it served nonetheless as a useful disclaimer for anything that people didn't wholly agree with. And with this particular incident, the 'exposure' accusation was being passed back and forth between both camps, as sure a sign as any that neither side fully understood the actions of the other.

As Allan saw it, 'Both Chloe-Jane and Malia were stealing for their own gain. They'd done it just to get themselves on TV. Now, Malia, yes, is a vegetarian. But the day before this all happened, we'd caught a shark and she'd been running around with it on her back like a rucksack, so she's not *that* animal-friendly. And Chloe-Jane's not even a vegetarian anyway, so I could only conclude that she wanted to get herself some television time by doing all this.' Chloe-Jane, for her part, says, 'I think Allan slightly misunderstood the whole idea behind the goat thing – I'm not entirely sure he didn't just use it as an excuse to leave. He said he saw me in the same light as Genevieve, because I'd stolen from the group. But he was the only one to see it that way.' Troubled by the moral dilemma, Allan approached Chloe-Jane to discuss it. 'I mean, we were never on bad terms because of it,' he insists, 'but I said, "I'm sorry, it's stealing – I'm going to have to nominate you to be thrown off the island". And she said, "Yeah, I thought you probably would. We knew what we were getting ourselves into."'

So I went and nominated them, but I sort of knew that the group weren't going to go for it. Anyone who'd voted for Genevieve to stay had to vote for Chloe-Jane and Malia to stay as far as I was concerned, but by the same token, anyone who voted for Genevieve to *go* had to vote for these two to go. Anything else would have been unfair on Genevieve. I mean, I was never a fan of Genevieve in the first place, but once you've set a precedent, you have to stick with it. So I put the nomination forward, went into HutCam and made the nomination, but pointed out that if they weren't expelled, I'd nominate myself. If they were going to be that unfair to someone, that hypocritical, I just didn't want to be there any more.

As a test of the laws they'd created for themselves, the nomination would, as Allan already knew, fail at the first hurdle. 'Oh, I was well aware that it wouldn't happen,' he confirms. 'Not enough people would vote for them to leave, as Chloe-Jane and Malia were much more popular than Genevieve ever was.' Which sheds a different, and not entirely favourable light on the process leading to Genevieve's expulsion, when you think about it. For all the talk of stealing, of trust, of the need to protect the group as a whole, it suddenly being suggested that at least part of the decision had come down to a matter of popularity. Possibly recognizing the flaws in the group's earlier decision, then, Allan was very firm about standing by the standards they'd set for themselves. But, as he wrote in his diary, it was far from being a clear-cut issue:

The problem was, am I prepared to leave the island on the basis of a principle? Or more to the point, am I prepared *not* to? Both paths lead only to regret, so it's a question of deciding which one will hurt me the most. I knew when I nominated them that it effectively meant I would be leaving

ALLAN BRIDGES

the island the next morning. Realizing that I can stand up and be accounted for is part of it. It hurts like hell, but I can't stop myself. Whatever my feelings towards Genevieve may be, I'd made the decision to nominate her, and have since taken the hard line whenever anyone has spoken about stealing. To back down now isn't an option.

As Allan predicted, the vote went in favour of Chloe-Jane and Malia staying. When he then requested to be voted off the island himself, the others refused initially, although after much soul-searching and explanation, the reluctant decision was made formal.

After lunch, I went back to the beach to sunbathe and enjoy my last few hours on Yaukuvelevu. I'd come to terms with my decision and certainly held no ill will towards Malia and Chloe-Jane. At the end of a great day, the best I'd had on Yaukuvelevu, I had nothing but good thoughts for everyone who had shared my time there. My last sunset was a fantastic one. I stood and stared at it for fully twenty minutes and realized how much I was giving up. I was choking back tears again. But as I trudged off to bed, I realized that I had just had one of the best days ever. The perfect note to be leaving on.

The following day, Allan woke early and – a writer to the end – penned goodbye notes to his fellow castaways:

I tried to sum up what they had all come to mean to me, but I'm sure I didn't manage it. I cherish every argument, every silence, every chore, just as much as any one of the great moments. Right now, I'd like to live here forever. After writing the letters, I strolled along the beach and realized that this is the best way to live. In a society where greed doesn't exist. Which sounds like I've got my head up my bum, but the fact is, it's true. And I've come to realize I've been a selfish git in England.

When the boat finally arrived, hugs were exchanged, letters handed out, and the enormity of the decision suddenly dawned on Allan. 'Christ, this is hard,' he wrote. 'I'm trying to put on a brave face, making inept jokes about how good it is to be going. It isn't. I've only got feelings of regret about making my stance as I get on the boat, and tears are just a few footsteps away. As the boat pulls away, the tears come. There was no way to stop them, I didn't even try.'

Back in England, with his emotions settled again, Allan was asked if he still regretted the decision. There followed a long sigh. 'I'll tell you what was strange,' he finally says, 'I was back on Fiji with Randy and Leon, and at that point I was gutted. While they were saying they were so glad to be off the island, and how the whole thing had been rubbish, I was saying, "No, it was brilliant." I just thought, "Well that's it, one of the best experiences of my life and it's over." If I'm absolutely honest, I regretted the situation, but not the decision.'

I had a great time out there and would drop everything to go back out there and with exactly the same people. Wouldn't hesitate to. I'd love it. It was one hundred per cent worthwhile – I was drifting along before I went out there, and suddenly I was having the most amazing experience of my life. It was so surreal. That last night on Fiji before leaving for England, I was watching the sunset again, and all that I could think about was that they would all be watching the same sunset over on Yaukuvelevu. I was wondering what they were thinking and what they'd be doing that night. And I wondered if I'd ever again be as happy as I was there. And the answer's 'Probably not.' Let's face it, it's pretty difficult to top perfection.

7

MALIA
WALSH

Age: 20
Profession: 'Bar-chick'
Luxury Item: Fire-dancing equipment

We all know that using stereotypes to label people is bad. But let's be honest, that doesn't stop us doing it. It's easy, it's convenient, but more importantly, pretty much all stereotypes have some element of truth to them, however small that element may be.

In that regard, Melbourne-born Malia, while boasting one of the most complex and arguably most misunderstood personalities of all the castaways, was also a pretty good illustration of the cultural differences that exist between the English and the Australians. Before we get to that, though, let's look at the labels she predicted she'd attract, even before setting foot on the island. 'When people watch the show on television, they'll probably see me as the alterna-chick,' she laughed. 'I mean, I'd like to be seen as the nice, fun girl, the intelligent one with the really great personality, but I think the only thing people will notice is that I'm the girl with the hairy armpits.'

As it turned out, she wasn't far off the mark. Even at the Australian selection weekend, the crew had jotted down a few notes about her idiosyncratic approach to body hair, describing her as a 'flame-throwing feminist, with hairy pits and legs, pink hair and the bluest of eyes.' They also called her, and not without good reason, 'a primal sex symbol'. When word of that reached Malia, she just fell about laughing: '"Primal sex symbol?" I *love* that. I've got to get that printed on a T-shirt!'

Randy, for one, would agree. In a very sweet letter to Malia, he told her how much her beauty had grown on him over their time together on the island. 'It grew more as your body hair grew,' he wrote. 'Which is funny, because I never thought I'd be attracted to a girl with underarm hair. If there's one thing that I'll take away from this experience, it's that crap like that doesn't matter.'

Definitely a 'do-er' rather than a 'talker', Malia was as shocked as all the others by the conditions on Yaukuvelevu. As we've already seen, the response to those conditions pretty much divided out into two camps: those who let it get to them, and those who didn't. Malia fell immediately, and very firmly into the second camp. 'I was a bit shocked to find out that we weren't going to get any ration deliveries,' she admitted, 'but I took the positive side – you know, I just thought "Great, this is an added bonus." This whole experience is something that I've always wanted to do. I've always wanted to live off the land, so as far as I was concerned, this was fabulous.'

A better example of the old saying 'If life gives you lemons, make lemonade' you'd be hard pressed to find, but, as Malia soon discovered, that particular approach wasn't shared by everyone out there. 'I was really excited about that whole "survival of the fittest" thing,' she reflects, 'but a lot of the English guys weren't interested in that aspect, which upset me quite a bit. I was like, "Come on guys, what are you here for?"'

That particular question is an interesting one. Each castaway had his or her reasons for being on the island, although the fact that the experience meant considerable TV exposure was one that each and every one of them mentioned prior to heading out.

With the exception of Malia. She's the first to admit that she's the product of hippy parents, and would repeatedly stress that 'living off the land is more important to me than being on the telly.' Some of the others found that a little hard to believe, particularly Allan, who described this whole 'I'm not in it for the fame' attitude as 'complete bull****. No one believed her, and everyone got really annoyed. Let's face it, no one likes a sanctimonious little Madam.' Harsh stuff, perhaps, but then as Malia is quick to point out, 'Allan's such a cynical bastard. He didn't really get involved in anything – he documented everything, sat on his arse and wrote about it, but didn't actually take part in that much.'

If you're beginning to form a picture of a no-nonsense, direct young woman, you wouldn't be far wrong. And it's here that we return to those national stereotypes. In the world of sweeping generalizations, the English have always considered the Australians to be blunt, to the point of utter tactlessness. Australians, in return, would argue that life's too short for tippy-toeing around on eggshells – they respect people who say what they mean and don't spend a lifetime getting to the point. On the other side of that particular coin, Australians have a phrase, 'whingeing Pom', which refers to the Brits' endless capacity to complain about anything that doesn't move or answer back.

In fairness, the only time Malia ever used that expression was when she referred to the cast of *Shipwrecked* series two. She'd seen a couple of episodes, and clearly remembered the British contingent moaning about their rice diet. You can pretty much understand, then, how after a ten-week diet consisting primarily of yams, she would come to view her *Shipwrecked* predecessors as 'a bunch of complete whingers'.

The Australian mindset, see, recognizes that complaining about a problem doesn't actually help to resolve it. Instead, your (stereo)typical Aussie prefers to get stuck in and actually *do* something about it. As Malia recalls, 'The English people used to go on about how horrible England is and it really astounded me. They'd be saying how crap it was, and I'd just say, "Well move, then! What are you there for?" They really didn't seem to understand that they were able to leave if they didn't like it.'

In the early weeks, when the 'English Girls' were conspicuously absent from the hard graft and more often than not, busy working on their tans, Malia was busying herself along with Chloe-Jane, Rainbow and the boys. As she wrote in her diary on Day 5:

> It's a different world out here, one where there's not much comfort, and not much choice. I can't choose whether I want to sit on the beach and sun myself or if I want to work in the veggie patch. Fact is, it *has* to be the veggie patch, otherwise I won't eat. It's as simple as that. Then again, I love it. My hands are brown from the dirt — it's so embedded that it doesn't wash off. I have cuts and bites all over me, my hair's dry, and I look like crap. But I feel amazing. I've lived on an island for five days with only water and pots and pans given to us. We've done so well, and it will only get better.

Fact is, Malia's positive outlook worked for others as well as for herself. While some of the castaways dealt with their hunger by constantly talking about the food they missed, she preferred to busy herself getting the food that was available. 'Everyone complained about yams being boring,' she recalls. 'I was just like, "Get over it, at least we're eating."' A good point well made, but a view that didn't make her many friends initially. As Jeffro saw it, 'Malia would have a go at people for talking about food, 'cos she was as hungry as the rest of us. But if you don't want to hear people talking about food, you walk away from the conversation, you don't have a go at them, do you?'

That said (and let's just remind ourselves that this whole experience is one littered with contradictions and rapidly evolving
opinions), Jeffro also respected Malia's views. On Day 16 he wrote:
'Something Malia said earlier today really made sense. What a star
she is – she just pointed out that if everyone stopped talking
about the things we *don't* have, the things we *used* to do back
home, and concentrated instead on what we have here, on the
people we're sharing the experience with, then we would have a
much better time now. Good shout, Sheila!'

Like Rainbow, Malia was a vegetarian before coming to the
island. And like Rainbow, she knew that this particular lifestyle
choice, while perfectly do-able in Western civilisation, would not
be a viable option on the island. After four years of not eating
meat, then, Malia would have little choice but to live off the island's
natural resources, and that, inevitably, would include the pigs and
the chickens. If it had to be done, it had to be done, but Malia
didn't take the decision lightly. On Day 5 she wrote, 'They've
decided to kill one of the pigs tomorrow. I don't honestly know
how I feel about that, but I've decided to get quite involved in the
planning, just because I don't want anything to get wasted. Maybe
I'll be sick if I eat it, I really don't know.'

The next day, by her own admission, Malia kept away from the
actual killing of the pig:

I must admit I was quite upset about it. The thought of it
made me sick. I just got on with making a bush-oven to
cook it in. Of course, the TV crew wanted to interview me,
because they probably see me as the typical, upset veggie. I
don't care about that, but I really hope they don't make me
out to be some sad wimp who'd burst into tears at the
sight of a crushed fly. F**k off, that's not me.

What *did* upset her, however, was the lack of respect shown to the dead animal, this being a theme that would recur throughout the ten weeks, and not only, it has to be said, in Malia's diary. On Day 19 she witnessed Leon and Salvo killing a shark, and found the event particularly troubling. 'I'm not happy with the way they dealt with it,' she wrote in her diary. 'I saw the fire in Salvo's eyes when he stabbed it. But what can you do? These boys have been blooded, all they talked about was what animal they should kill next. There's just no respect for life there, but I can't do anything – they're all so hungry for meat that they won't listen to reason. It's a strange world that I'm living in…'

A strange world? Bit of an understatement, that. And while we've already had an insight into the 'survival' side of things, the difference it makes when you can't just pop out to the supermarket, there's another side of things that might seem less vital than the quest for food, but which, in its own way, is just as important: entertainment. Think about it a while. We can't begin to put ourselves in the shoes of these people, but just try to imagine a world with no radio, no television, no cinema, no videos, no nightclubs. In short, a world where the only entertainment you get is what you make for yourself. Most of us would find it hard enough to get through one weekend of that, much less ten weeks.

That particular gap was neatly filled by the castaways' judicious choice of luxury items. Geordie brought a guitar, Rainbow formed the rhythm section with her drums, while Malia provided the visuals with her fire-dancing. Anyone who saw the closing ceremony of the Sydney 2000 Olympics, in fact, will already have witnessed her fire-dancing skills – then only nineteen, Malia was not just a participant, but also a supervisor in the show that closed the games, a spectacle that was rightly considered one of the finest in Olympic history. 'That was pretty amazing,' she beams. 'Having ten thousand people cheering and screaming around you… just incredible.'

The castaways were privileged to witness their own perform-ance on Jeffro's birthday. Now this, in fairness, is one event you *have* to see on the television show, as words will only go so far in describing the event. That said, Allan's description, as written down in one of his many diaries, is as clear a picture as language offers. 'I was dumbstruck,' he wrote. 'I knew that she'd be good – she'd been selected to do this at the Olympics, after all – but I'd never seen anything like it before. Sat on a tropical beach at night, with millions of stars across the sky, sitting around a huge campfire, slightly merry… I just sat there with my mouth wide open, unable to even clap. I was mesmerized, and I won't ever forget it.' Jeffro, for his part, agreed. 'It was the most amazing thing I'd ever seen. She really was excellent.'

Later on in the stay, Salvo – who was never frightened to put his hand to any new challenge that presented itself – would provide his own, rather less elegant version of fire-dancing, one that would leave the poor boy with a nasty burn in a particularly sensitive area. More on that later, but it's worth mentioning here that in addition to genital burns, our Sicilian friend was party to another *Shipwrecked* exclusive.

As Malia explains, 'Before I went to the island, my mum told me that I wasn't allowed to show my tits on television, I wasn't allowed to have sex with anyone, and I wasn't allowed to fall in love with someone and move to another country with them.' And in the fine tradition of 'Two out of three ain't bad', Malia managed only the last two. 'I flashed at Salvo once,' she admits, laughing. 'Sorry, but it had to be done. The guy was always walk-ing about with nothing on, so I thought, 'Right sweetie, you're gonna get it' and he freaked out completely – didn't know what to do. It was fabulous.'

He may have been freaked out, but that state didn't last long. Towards the end of the stay, Salvo wrote a note to Malia in her diary: 'Hi Malia, you are the most beautiful girl on the island and you have gorgeous, beautiful breasts. I like them so much!' However, there was a more serious side to Salvo's attitude towards women that she found altogether less acceptable. As she explained, 'The gender divisions that arose on the island were pretty much down to Salvo being a sexist pig most of the time. You know, he'd say "Oh, you can't do this, you're not strong enough" and I think that really played on a lot of the girls' minds.'

You might, by this point, be getting the impression (as indeed, many of the castaways did) that Malia was a little stroppy at times. Throughout the diaries, the others described her on more than one occasion as 'a bitch'. But by the same token, it's pretty much accepted these days that 'bitch' is just a word that people use for a woman who knows how to speak her own mind and isn't afraid to do so. And if that's the case, Malia would be proud to wear the crown. When things upset her, she said so, and in no uncertain terms. Like all the other castaways, Malia was prone to the highest highs and the lowest lows, although looking back on the experience, she admits that she hid her feelings for much of the time:

I didn't want to be this screaming, emotional nutcase on camera. I didn't want to bitch and complain, because that really drives me up the wall. But I almost wish I had, because there were a lot of things I wish I'd said to some people. The most irritating thing was that people didn't understand me. I don't think any of them took me that seriously. And there were little things that could annoy you so much. Vicki would wear a watch and I just didn't get that. We're on a desert island – it's not like dinner's going to be called at twelve! It drove me insane, because every half an hour they'd be asking each other what time it was. Drove me up the wall. I thought the whole idea was to remove yourself from civilization — you know, just living, breathing and forgetting all that crap that society makes you do.

She claims to have changed relatively little over the course of her stay on Yaukuvelevu, but is aware of one lesson it taught her. 'I got a big insight into people,' she admits, 'but, if anything, that made me more negative about them. At home you have such a wide choice of friends, and I surround myself with people who are like me, and share my beliefs. I don't know whether that's a good or bad thing. On the island I was thrown together with people I wouldn't normally talk to. It's strange getting to know people you wouldn't normally want to know. And on such a deep level as well.' She frowns for a moment. 'Actually, the more I think about it, I *have* changed. I feel a lot older. I'm harder and I think a lot more. Before I went out there I was the sort of person who'd be dancing on tables in clubs, making a spectacle of myself. Now I'm a little more reserved, which is scary — everyone thinks I'm getting boring.'

Malia also had less time for what she now refers to as 'the island games'. Partly, it could be argued, because she was less concerned than others by the television side of things, but partly because, well, that's just how she is. Take the hierarchy system, for example: 'We voted in a leader every week, but they weren't the real leaders in my opinion. It was more like voting in a Prom King or Queen — who was the most popular for that week. It was such a load of crap, and it really pissed me off. The real leaders were the people everyone looked up to, and that was Geordie and Salvo, I guess.' Excuse me? Salvo? 'Yes, Salvo,' she laughs. 'As much as he was obnoxious, he knew things, and people would always be asking him what to do.'

But going back to that old lemons/lemonade thing, Malia made sure she got what she wanted out of the island:

I was so happy over there. I didn't really want to go home. Going home meant having to settle down and get a job, and I wasn't really looking forward to that. I wanted to hide out on the island for a little more. Looking back, there were so many perfect times, it's hard to pin down a favourite. It just happened that the cameras weren't around for most of my favourite moments. All those times sitting on the beach, bonding with a couple of the others, opening a coconut and talking all night... you can't really capture something like that on film.

As for her immediate plans, it'll come as no surprise to learn that she's already getting itchy feet back in Melbourne, and is looking forward to travelling around Europe in the near future. 'Oh, and I'm planning on throwing a *Shipwrecked* party,' she laughs. 'When people walk through the door, they get sprayed with dirt and sand, then I'll make them open a coconut and feed them grilled yam.'

And as far as those nasty telly people go?

I'm honestly pleased that they made it harder. That's the main part of the experience – I'd wake up in the morning, walk from my hut to the bathroom and I knew where every single stone on the path was – I could do it with my eyes closed. Yaukuvelevu showed me the excessiveness of how we live at home – we eat more than we need, we use more than we need. It's made me want to put something back, to remind people of beauty, to remind them to live just that little bit more. That's something I'd never trade.'

8

SARAH-JANE CRAWFORD

Age: 19
Profession: Fashion student
Luxury Item: Hot chocolate

'I've always been the kind of person who thinks "Yeah, I could do that," but without having any real concept of the work involved,' admitted Sarah-Jane on her return to England from Yaukuvelevu.

In some ways, that's a good thing, because it means I don't end up denying myself challenges, but once you find yourself doing it, it's like 'Oh my *god*...' and that was how it was with *Shipwrecked*. I'd seen the other two series, and I'd thought, 'Yeah, I can handle that' but I had *no* idea how tough it was going to be. On the training island, I was anticipating our arrival on Yaukuvelevu and I was actually scared at that point: it dawned on me that this would be the first time that I had been in a situation that I had absolutely no control over. I just thought, 'Everything's going to have to be done from scratch', and that was what I was concerned about. But that's what happens when you go around saying 'Yeah, I can do that.'

Like she says, though, it's the kind of approach that opens up challenges, and while she's modestly matter-of-fact about her achievements on the island, Sarah-Jane not only met that challenge head-on, but she also became the subject of one of the most impressive success stories that the series has ever introduced to the viewing public. Both cast and crew remarked that they'd never seen a person change so much, and so much for the better.

So what went right? And what went wrong?

When I got there, my immediate approach was, 'OK, you've got to do what you can to survive this'. I had an 'Everyone for themselves' kind of attitude, I think. At that stage, I didn't see the point of doing things as a group, to be honest, because it seemed like a lot more effort, and with very little reward. So if you went into the woods and two of you found a papaya, which happened with me and Vicki, you're going to get a lot more out of it by sharing it between the two of you. But everyone else's mentality was 'Everything's got to be split sixteen ways, no matter how small it is.'

The first week, it goes without saying, was not the happiest of times for Sarah-Jane. 'The first couple of days were such a struggle that I couldn't really see myself lasting,' she recalls, 'much less staying for ten.' Before departing for the island, Sarah-Jane admitted that the material things she would miss most would be her bed ('I hate sleeping rough') and — being a fashion student — her make-up. Reminded of this when she returned to England, she simply howls with laughter: 'How pathetic! The funny thing is, Vicki and myself and a couple of the others were talking about how we were going to smuggle eyeliner and make-up onto the island. And we actually ended up putting this stuff into water bottles and so on, I can't believe how desperate we were! But within a week of arriving there I remember thinking, "Why did we bother doing that? This is *so* unimportant."'

Sarah-Jane had bonded with Vicki on the selection weekend, and the two of them, along with Genevieve, Gemma and Donna, soon formed the much-maligned and ill-fated 'English girls' clique, till Genevieve's expulsion from the island. Sarah-Jane's theory is that the whole thing could have been avoided: 'We were all saying when we were there, that if we'd had rations there from the beginning, like the last lot did, then Genevieve wouldn't have gone – everything was so much more intense and people were so much more emotional because of the lack of food. Every action seemed to have much bigger consequences than it would have done back at home.'

That said, even with Genevieve gone, the ramifications of her departure were still keenly felt by the remaining girls:

When the decision was made to get rid of her, I was really upset, because the last straw had been something that me, her, Vicki, Gemma and Donna had *all* been involved in, so I felt I played a big part in her being voted off. I was also really concerned that I'd be voted off in a couple of days' time – we had no idea what they'd all been planning, it was only a couple of minutes before the meeting that they told us. They were so sure about their decision, though – I don't think anything would have changed their mind at that point.

As Sarah-Jane explains, though, certain members of the group used the event to create a culture of fear among the remaining girls:

You had Salvo wandering around saying, 'If you don't work, we throw you off too.' It turned into a bit of a witch-hunt, actually, and for a short period back then it really became my biggest fear, that I would get expelled. I'm glad I didn't let it completely overtake my experience, because I'd have just ended up sitting there being very quiet, being very careful what I said to certain people. Luckily, when I gained a bit more respect from the group, that allowed me to be myself, but yes, there was definitely a point where I was just thinking 'Oh my god, it's going to be me next.' Things did change after Genevieve left, though, and for the better. I'm not sure what actually triggered that – I think it may have had more to do with coincidence than anything else.

Part of that change involved the shaking off of the 'lazy' label that had been slapped onto the English girls. 'At the very beginning,' she explains, 'everyone's OK with each other, because they don't know one another that well. And then about two weeks in or so, the first opinions are formed, and people start acting according to the opinion that they've formed of you. And if they've decided they don't respect you, that's it, that's how they're going to treat you.'

With all the girls taking a more hands-on approach to the day-to-day work on the island, it still seemed that some of the other castaways were going to be harder to impress than others. In one of the most bizarre moments from the TV series, you'll see Sarah-Jane cooking a meal of fried yams for the others while Salvo sits nearby watching. His reaction? To criticize her for being lazy. While she's cooking and he's doing... well, nothing. But then, reason and logic were never going to stop Salvo getting something off his chest, and it's to her credit that Sarah-Jane – who, don't let's forget, had a bowl of hot oil at her disposal – just carried on with her work, effectively ignoring Salvo, until he had no option but to storm off in one of his soon-to-be famous petulant paddies. Sarah-Jane – 1, Salvo – 0.

Sarah-Jane laughs when she thinks back to the confrontation:

The thing is, I'm just not like that at all. Normally I would have blown up, don't let there be any mistake about that. But some people had said to me, 'Look, why don't you practise not letting him get to you and see what happens.' Which was a pretty tall demand, but that was my first lesson in Ignoring Salvo! I'll be honest with you, there was definitely a stage where I felt like leaving the island, and it was all because of Salvo and the way he made me feel. In the camp it was always Sarah-Jane versus Salvo. Everyone was aware of it and commented on it – they couldn't understand why I let him get away with it. The thing is, because he's such a dominant character it gave people the impression that I was in some way submissive.

People change, however, and it wasn't long before a peace of sorts was reached between the two of them. 'I think the stage where it changed was when he had a huge flare-up towards the others in the group, and they began to see what I was putting up with,' explains Sarah-Jane. 'In particular he had a massive argument with Shawn, and after that he realized that he was upsetting people and he learned to apologize. In fairness, Salvo had me in stitches at times, but at times I wanted to kill him. The way he used to fight for attention the whole time was incredible.'

Already, the need to adapt to this weird self-made community was becoming apparent to Sarah-Jane. She'd thrown herself into the work, and had even been voted to go on the ration run to the neighbouring island of Dravuni, in recognition of that work. And that, like pretty much every event on the island, was not a simple matter. As in past series, *everyone* wanted to be on that boat, places were limited, and not everyone was happy with the final team of Randy, Sarah-Jane, Chloe-Jane, Simon, and Rainbow. The nominations had been made on the basis that the crew who'd gone to the neighbouring island on Jeffro's birthday would not be eligible for the ration run, a decision accepted by all the castaways at the time.

When Geordie suggested on 6 June that the weather was good enough to make the run, not everyone immediately agreed, as Sarah-Jane recalls:

> Chloe-Jane felt that if we tried to do the run we would fail without a doubt, and that this would only provide certain other members of the group with ammunition to demand a change in crew and so get themselves on the run through the back door. And as it transpired, she was right. The first attempt was a disaster; with the wind and current against us, we just went nowhere. And sure enough, when we got back to camp we were greeted by Leon and Salvo. Not an official meeting, but they still had plenty to say. Leon started by subtly suggesting that certain people on the crew be replaced, namely Rainbow and myself.

Now, you'll recall that both Leon and Salvo had had their bit of high-seas adventure with Jeffro's birthday treasure-map. In other words, a desperate measure was being attempted to rewrite the rules, and Sarah-Jane for one, was having none of it, as she described in her diary:

> His tone was so patronizing, but also really aggressive. He argued that he was fully aware that we would all fail, and that his reason for encouraging us to go out in the wrong conditions, was simply because he wanted us to wake up to a few 'home truths'. After about five minutes of this spiel, I just lost it. 'What the hell do you mean by that?!' I shouted, and that was it, we were both shouting at each other. It

would seem, unfortunately, that at this point in my life, I cannot last long in an argument without crying. I've noticed that since I've been on the island, I've been more vulnerable and very sensitive.

Asked how she felt about her tears being captured on camera, she shrugs: 'The cameras were kind of incidental, after a while. People told me before I went out that I'd forget they were there. The thing is, you're never going to be one hundred per cent natural in front of a camera unless you're in the middle of a huge row and nothing matters.' Like everyone else, she had to learn to live with it, although, 'The only time the cameras got to me was on the days when I was really upset. If there was a bit of emotion, they wanted to catch it on film — I could understand that, and you obviously couldn't turn around and say "Leave me alone", but I did find that a bit hard at times.'

It was by now an unspoken island tradition that when a castaway was upset, he or she should find a nice quiet patch of beach and gather themselves together, which is precisely what Sarah-Jane did:

I went off to calm down, and Jeffro came and found me and we ended up having a chat. I just explained that I felt a lot of people in the group didn't respect me and I wasn't entirely sure why. Well actually, I think I kind of knew why, but I felt a little bit paralysed and frustrated because I didn't seem able to turn it around. So Jeffro pointed out that none of them really knew me, but that was because I was spending all my time with Vicki and people just came to see us as a joint package. He said I had to let them get to know Sarah-Jane, rather than just 'Sarah-Jane-and-Vicki', and that they'd respect me more as an individual. Which makes perfect sense.

The other stroke of genius in Jeffro's plan was to tell Sarah-Jane to actively seek out the people she didn't get on with, and do chores with them. Before long, this led – however improbable it may sound – to Leon and Sarah-Jane going off to dig yams together. As Sarah-Jane recalls, 'After about five minutes, Leon turned round and said, "I'm glad we got this opportunity to talk." He suggested that our best way forward was to talk abut ourselves as individuals, rather than pinpointing the things we didn't like in each other. After a while, we were getting on really well! Yes! The plan's worked!'

It was a key moment in the way that Sarah-Jane was perceived by the others, and slowly they started noting that change in their diaries. As Chloe-Jane observed, 'Sarah, as a person, improved tenfold. She came home a totally different person. I don't know how many of the others noticed it, but it was very apparent to me. She was excellent.' A sense that 'New Sarah-Jane' had arrived was keenly felt by all, but even so, when it came to the second attempt on the ration run, someone stepped in once more with other plans. *HMS Spencer* having been destroyed by storms, a new raft had been constructed, one that would only carry two people. Of their own accord, both Rainbow and Sarah-Jane stepped down from the run. A new ballot was held with Chloe-Jane and Randy emerging as the new ration-run crew.

Simon, though, had other plans. Deeply disappointed by his exclusion from the run, he set about building a second boat. Loosely described as a canoe, it was 'more of a log'; if Sarah-Jane's word is anything to go by. He announced to the others that he'd constructed a three-man boat, immediately prompting Malia to announce, 'Oh good – then the girls *can* go.' Which seems only fair, but Simon had other ideas: 'Nah, Jeffro and Geordie,' he said. No vote, no discussion. As was only fit and proper, a huge argument ensued with – once things had calmed down – an unofficial meeting deciding that since Rainbow had an injured hand, it would be best for Shawn and Sarah-Jane to man the new boat.

It had already been a long, and argument-packed journey, even before they'd so much as set off, but as Sarah-Jane recalls:

> The ration run was such a highlight. Even though I nearly drowned! I'd actually let on that I was more of a competent swimmer than I really am, and you can see me struggling in the water — but I had my lifejacket on and everything, it's not like I was going to be allowed to sink! Simon was so fired up about it, and was so determined to get across no matter what. And I was just happy to be going. But it was one of the hardest things I've ever done in my life — we were rowing solid for three hours. I had no idea that it was going to be that hard.

The other raft (manned by Chloe-Jane and Randy) was significantly lighter than Simon's boat, and Sarah-Jane and Simon eventually started falling behind, to a point at which they risked losing contact with the other two. With their destination in sight, eventually the four decided that it would be best for all of them to use the raft — two actually on it, two holding on to it. At this point, it's perhaps worth mentioning that one of the things that had originally worried Sarah-Jane about island life was the prospect of coming across a shark. As it happened, they were briefly troubled by a sea-snake, which turned out to be of a non-venomous variety, but as she recalls, 'The next thirty minutes were physically and mentally the hardest time I have ever been through in my whole life.'

Finally, they arrived at the beach. 'We must have looked like something out of *Robinson Crusoe*,' wrote Sarah-Jane. 'We were dripping wet, and freezing. But I felt the most massive sense of achievement – we all did. And I had the most wonderful time on Dravuni. The locals actually cried when we walked into their community hall – it was incredibly emotional and very humbling, and their hospitality was absolutely breathtaking. They made us coffee and papaya jam and butter on crackers, which tasted amazing.'

On her return to Yaukuvelevu, the next challenge that faced Sarah-Jane was that of being group leader for the penultimate week, although she was thrilled at her election. 'I felt that it showed just how much progress I'd made within the group,' she beams, 'that all my efforts had been recognized.' She confessed to being worried that, this late in the day, there'd be little for her to actually *do* while in charge of the group. As it turned out, Chloe-Jane and Malia's goat-liberation and Allan's subsequent departure meant that she had more than enough on her hands for that week.

Back in England, Sarah-Jane remains justifiably proud of her island experience. 'The two weeks when it rained constantly were a real low point,' she concedes, 'but purely from a practical point of view. We didn't have any real shelter, we had no dry clothes, and you're thinking, "Please let me go home." The mood of the group was definitely weather-dependent.'

Apart from the harshness of day-to-day island life, the thing that surprised Sarah-Jane most was realizing how much other people mattered to her:

I didn't have any idea how much I would miss my family, and how having no contact with them would affect me. I thought I'd be fine, because I've lived away from home for a couple of years, but I realized while I was over there just how much you take for granted in terms of relationships. In a way, being on the island is a bit like being in prison – you've got so much time on your hands and you're just thinking how much you could be doing. I've noticed since I got back that I can't sit around any more – I have to be doing something all the time.

And that wasn't the only change she noticed. 'It was really strange sleeping in my own bed after all that time,' she laughs. 'You get so used to the sound of the sea at night, and then back at home it just seems really silent. And I felt really alone as well – I'd spent the last ten weeks sleeping in a group, and suddenly it feels strange to be on your own. I went down to London a couple of days after I got back, on the underground, in the West End, and I just thought, "Whoah – this is weird. All these *people*!"'

All told, Sarah-Jane remains grateful for the experience, and for what it did for her, although she was very quick to add:

I'm glad to be back. The other day I had a massive argument with my family and I went to my room and was just thinking, 'If only I could go down to the other end of the beach.' Things are so much easier when you can just set up camp. The nice thing about it is, I don't miss it *terribly*. Everything had progressed towards a natural point, and I think it was time for us to go. I look back with really fond memories, but not wishing I was back there. If I'd left the island without gaining the rest of the group, then maybe I would have been looking back with regret, but everything seemed so complete when I left.'

9

RANDY WAYNE
FREDERICK

Age: 19
Profession: Model/Actor
Luxury Item: An American football

For an insight into the refreshing honesty of youth, look no further than the youngest male castaway, Randy. And before you ask, yes, this young Californian is well aware of the connotation of his name in English culture. Asked about his reasons for going to the island, he initially claimed: 'I'm not really expecting anything from this – I'm doing it for fun and out of a sense of accomplishment.' Which is all very commendable and all that, but casually mention the fact that he'll be sharing the island with eight bikini-clad girls, and his face just breaks into the hugest grin. 'Girls?' he beams. 'That's one of the main reasons I'm going. There's going to be, like, seven or eight hot chicks there. At the American selection weekend, I got the "Most likely to make out" award. It's a big island, you can get away... it'll happen. You'll see, I promise.'

Brave words, but then Randy isn't short of confidence. 'I think at first I can come across as arrogant when people don't know me,' he warns, 'but as they get to know me better, I think they realize it's just confidence, and that I'm a really friendly guy.' Talking about the island ordeal that faced him, he asserted, 'I'm one hundred per cent positive that I'll stay the course. When I was a kid I was always taught to stick with things to the end. Like, American football – I really wasn't too fond of it, but my mom wouldn't let me quit. I've always been raised to finish what I started.'

And having started to talk about his future success with the ladies, Randy pronounced himself *extremely* happy on arrival at Yaukuvelevu:

> I'd already met Malia and Rainbow before we got to Yaukuvelevu and I wasn't really attracted to either of them to start with, so as we were approaching the island, I was thinking, 'Damn, I hope there's some hot girls here.' Then I saw Vicki and Gemma and Sarah-Jane and I thought, 'That's it, it's going down. I'm going to use up all those condoms there, I'm in heaven!' A deserted island with these beautiful girls and they've got nowhere to run to? I was sure I was going to get laid. Gemma just had to smile, and that was it – her smile is amazing. She could be a supermodel, no problems.

The warmth of the international welcome, however, would not last much longer that day. To celebrate the arrival of the Australians and Americans on the island, a party was held down at the beach. This being the first party to include all the castaways, it provided a chance for all of them to get to know each other and indulge in some moonlit bonding. In theory. In practice, however, it resulted in Randy getting involved (reluctantly, it must be stressed) in a fight on his first night on Yaukuvelevu. 'All the Brits had drunk their alcohol already,' he explains, 'but I had some, the Australians had some, so we broke it open and said, "OK, let's sing a bit, have a drink, get to know each other and have a bit of a party."'

'So everyone was getting along fine,' he continues, 'and then Simon started hitting the Jack Daniels. He became the life and soul of the party, singing and dancing, getting a bit crazy. Then he stood up in front of everyone and said, "No one in the world can pin me for three seconds." So I said, "Um, I can." And he said, "You Americans think you can come here and fix everything, think that you're going to take over. If you pin me, I'll give you my meals for the next two days.'"

Randy stresses that he wasn't even interested in making a bet out of it, partly because he was just playing around and partly because he knew he had an immediate advantage:

I used to wrestle for junior high, so I pretty much knew I could do it. So I stood up, started clapping my hands slowly, you know, just building up the atmosphere and having some fun with it. Then I just took him down and pinned him flat, and left it at that. Then he gets up and starts shouting, 'You didn't pin me, my shoulders weren't down, come on, let's go again.' And I couldn't be bothered then, I could see he was in danger of getting out of hand. At that point I had my back to him and he pushed me. Now usually I'm very laid-back, but when I get angry, I really get angry – I'm surprised I didn't hit him, but I just tackled him again and threw him down. We both landed in the fire, and then the others jumped in and pulled us apart. But even then he was still going on, saying he was going to slit my throat. And he wanted to wrestle *again*, so I just said, 'Look, I got lucky back there, you could beat me any time you wanted,' and left it at that.

As a pacifying technique it worked well, and even after this less-than-cordial reception, Randy insisted that he hadn't felt troubled. 'I never hold a grudge, ever,' he says, 'and I just thought the next day it would all be cool. The next morning he was still drunk! Still mad at everyone. And you know what, he didn't even drink that much.' Whereas Randy remained largely unbothered by the events, Simon's behaviour had certainly caught the attention of other members of the group. Allan noted in his diary, 'I'm not going to go into too much detail, suffice to say that things like, "Slit my throat, I don't care!" and "I've got to knock someone out" rang through the air for a while afterwards. Simon had basically ruined a great night for everyone. I spoke with Chloe-Jane and we decided that this was the only time we would put up with this type of thing. Next time, it would mean eviction, and I would lead the voting myself. He had scared people with his behaviour and that wasn't fair in such a small community.'

Of course, it didn't come to this, and Simon's behaviour from that day on would significantly change for the better, as everyone observed. Randy, for his part, was just happy that peace had been restored, although he would go on to create a few more diplomatic ripples (again, quite unintentionally) when he conducted a poll asking the castaways exactly what they thought of each other. As he explains:

At schools in America we have 'Superlatives'. Every high school votes for 'Best-looking', 'Best-dressed', 'Best couple', 'Most athletic', that kind of thing, so I did a similar thing on the island. And it wasn't about who was most popular, it was simply because I was interested to know what other people think. I don't care if they judge me, but I'm interested to know how they perceive me and each other. It's like anywhere – you get cliques. And on the island there were immediately cliques, which was part of the reason for the survey – that was me trying to get to know everybody. And I didn't show anybody [the results], so it wasn't like I was trying to cause trouble.

With the best will in the world, though, the project was bound to cause some ructions. Indeed, the whole concept was one that Rainbow found particularly unfair and demeaning. 'I feel as though I'm in high school again,' she wrote. 'Everyone's asking people who they fancy most, and the boys are all saying Vicki and Gemma. Salvo's going on about how his perfect girl has "dark hair, green eyes, a great ass like Vicki and great breasts like Vicki". I started to feel very unattractive, and the shallow way of assessing people saddened me. Sometimes the men on this island make men look bad.'

That said, even her earliest impressions of her male compatriots had been less than favourable, as Rainbow readily confirmed: 'When I first met Randy and Shawn,' she recalls, 'I'd really been hoping that they were going to be cool, but at the airport they were just checking out girls' asses and saying they wanted a piece of that and so on. They were like high-schoolers.' However, for all the 'phwoaring' there was a less-visible side to Randy's affections, one that went a little deeper than merely fixating on the visuals. His fondness for Gemma was very clear from his diary, in which he wrote, 'I was telling Gemma how easily she could make it as a model – she could do it in no time. I told her she could stay in California with me while she knocked on all the doors. But even if she never pursues that, her smile and personality will get her far in life. She's truly caring and so far from superficial. Uh oh… I feel an attraction coming on…'

With Gemma soon to depart, however, Randy was forced to turn his attentions elsewhere, and part of that shift in focus led to the game of Porno cards mentioned in Vicki's chapter. As Vicki notes, the guys involved (Randy and Salvo) stuck to a different, and perhaps more lurid version of events than the one *she* recalled, and indeed Randy's description of the evening does differ somewhat from her own. 'I really thought something was going to happen that night between me and the two girls,' he grins, 'but

Salvo muscled in on it and wouldn't leave, and there was no way I was going to do anything in front of him. When we got down to four cards, Salvo and I started cheating a little bit...'

All harmless fun, of course, but it still leaves the question why the castaway 'Most likely to make out' still hadn't managed to earn that label:

> You know what, I was so convinced that Vicki and me would do it before leaving the island, and after that night I was *sure* of it. But I still wasn't in the mood for it – which really bugs me, because I'm a horny guy: I'm Randy by name *and* nature! I know now that if we'd had food, it would have happened. Basically, none of us could get it up out there. I mean, I was sitting next to Sarah-Jane one day and she had her top off and I just didn't even care! And that's *so* not like me.

Day 36 on Yaukuvelevu saw the unannounced arrival of a high-profile outsider. And while to the British contingent, the sight of T4's Andi Peters walking up the beach was a faintly surreal, if most welcome vision, it's understandable that the non-English element were perhaps a little underwhelmed by the surprise. 'The Brits were going *nuts*,' Randy chuckled. 'Simon had a pillow, and gave it to Andi to sit on – and believe me, Simon wouldn't ever let anyone else sit on that pillow! I just thought, "Let him sit on the log like the rest of us!" I introduced myself to him and to begin with we didn't really hit it off. I understand English humour completely, even Allan admits that I do, but I just couldn't make Andi laugh. And that's the worst thing, to tell a joke and get no response.'

Andi had not arrived empty-handed, though. 'He pulled out some chocolate bars, and then some fizzy drink, a sort of lemon-lime thing,' grins Randy, 'and it was like we'd won the Lottery. At the time, it was the best drink I had ever tasted in my life. And the sugar rush! I tell you, I've seen people on cocaine and they don't even come close to the way we were. You want to get high? Eat nothing but yams for eight weeks then get yourself some sugar – you'll explode.'

In his diary, Randy described Andi's visit as 'the happiest moment on the island so far.' That sense of contentment, however, was only brief, and already Randy was having trouble with the idea of finishing his stay. Having, as he admitted, approached the whole *Shipwrecked* experience with little knowledge of the show, much less what to expect from it, he was finding it more of a trial than he'd anticipated. 'I really had been planning on having a good time out there,' he insists, 'but as time went on, by the second or third week I really started thinking hard about my best friend Kyle's wedding, which was coming up. We were hungry, bored, and arguing all the time, and I just thought, "No, this really isn't more important than being there on the most special day in his life."'

But the decision to escape was not one that was lightly entered into. As Randy revealed in his diary:

> I do not want to leave just yet – I want to stay to the end. It's really hard deciding what to do, but part of me really wants to remain here. I don't think this will help me publicity-wise, but friendship-wise, it will. And my friendship is more important to me than a reality TV show. They want reality? They're going to get it: they're going to see how much I want to be there for my friend's wedding. I can always get to England and party with these people again, but I'll never get a second chance to see Kyle exchange his vows.

Randy initially planned an escape with Shawn, who subsequently pulled out of the venture. His next choice of partner – Leon – came as a surprise to many of the others when they heard about it. All the more so when you learn that it was Randy who separated the Australian from his most beloved possession on the island:

Leon was really anal about his looks. Every day, first thing in the morning, Leon would be in front of the mirror for ten minutes. And as the day went by, he would still make a point of passing this little bitty green mirror that we had, just to check that he still looked all right. So one day I hid the mirror and put it in my backpack – and everyone immediately assumed that it was Leon, that he'd hidden it to keep for himself. So the mirror's gone, and at around the same time, it was noticed that tampons were being stolen. And three days later it was Jeffro's birthday. I gave him the rest of my liquor as a present, then pulled out the mirror and a toilet roll I'd made out of tampons. I'd stolen *all* the tampons and made him a toilet roll because I'm a nice kind of guy!

The fun and games weren't enough, though, and Randy finally decided to firm up his strategy for leaving Yaukuvelevu. The plan was simple enough: just to swim over to Dravuni island. That said, it was far from being a simple process, as Randy explained:

The day of the escape was crazy. We'd arranged to meet a local boatman, first thing in the morning. At that point, Salvo was going to come with us as well, just because Leon was going. We were all packed and ready, and had moved down to the beach to a corner where no one could see us. We waited forever, and no one came. No sign of the boatman at all, and the sun was already coming up. At that point Salvo decided not to bother, and wandered off back to camp. Then there was all this running around, and we worked out that CJ and Malia were setting the goat free.

Leon was really angry about that, but I thought it was pretty cool myself. But then there was the meeting, because Allan wanted to vote the girls off, then he wanted us to vote him off and it just went on and *on*. We really wanted to escape that day, but they just kept calling these damn meetings!

Finally, we got to leave. I'm not big on goodbyes, so we waited till the others were all having lunch before setting off. But they worked out that Leon and I were missing, so they ran down to the shore to wave us off – the only ones who weren't there were Salvo and Pierre. As for the escape itself – well, it was an easy swim, to be honest.

As Randy notes, the decision to escape had not been clear-cut in the early days, but by that point he was utterly convinced that he was doing the right thing. 'My reasoning was that I could either stay on the island for the next eight days and be bored and hungry like I had been,' he explains, 'or I could go to Dravuni, have all the food I wanted, see more of the Fijians and see how they lived. And that turned out to be fantastic. I had a great time with them – went to church with them every morning at 5.00am. I had the best time of my life there.'

Additionally, and perhaps oddly for a man whose career is based around being filmed and photographed, Randy had begun to find one aspect of Yaukuvelevu life particularly irritating: 'I actually got really sick of the cameras,' he says. 'I hid myself, and you won't see that much of me on the programme, I don't think. I did just as much as Salvo out there, but I didn't call the camera crew every time I wanted to climb a tree. Everyone was fighting for the camera's attention, and I just thought they looked like idiots, and I really didn't want to be part of that.'

And while Randy stresses that he liked both of his compatriots, he's already despairing of the PR job they've done for their country. Before going out to the island, he said that the idea of multinational communities didn't worry him at all. 'People are people, after all,' he had observed, 'and it shouldn't matter where you come from.' On leaving the island, however, he was quick to note that divisions of sorts had come about. 'Rainbow and Shawn are really cool outside of the island,' he insists, 'but on Yaukuvelevu they were impossible to get along with. It's worrying isn't it?' he frowns. 'Shawn and Rainbow are representatives of America and they're the most annoying people on the show! I just wanted to be the "normal American". You know what,' he adds. 'I think America will come out of this looking bad, so will Britain, but the Australians will look amazing. They were so cool.'

But even a dent in his national pride wasn't the most disappointing part of the experience for Randy. Ask him what he regrets most, and he pauses a while before responding. 'Hmm, I'd better be careful here – I guess it was the fact that I didn't get laid, but that doesn't sound very good, does it?' On a more positive note, the thing that impressed him most about his stay was 'the beauty of the island, and the clean air. My lungs had never felt so good. I learned a lot about England as well – and how to do the accents, so you never know when that might be useful in an acting career.' For the record, Randy can now do a spot-on Donna, Jeffro and Salvo.

But despite his misgivings, Randy pronounces himself very grateful for the experience, and certainly acknowledges the changes it's brought about in him. 'I've developed more patience,' he confirms, 'and a better understanding of people. I now understand that arguing isn't always the best thing to do. I really tried to keep peace out there, and I made some really good friends. I've taken away pretty much a whole new outlook on life.'

10

VICKI
BROOKS

Age: 19
Profession: Aspiring model
Luxury Item: Gas-powered hair-straightening tongs

No, that luxury item is *not* a misprint. Faced with ten gruelling weeks of hardcore survival, the then eighteen-year-old (Vicki would turn nineteen while on Yaukuvelevu) decided the thing that would best see her through was a pair of hair tongs. And if the word 'bimbo' is already forming in your mind, well, Vicki saw that label coming long before she'd even set off for the island:

> On the selection weekend, they were all saying, 'You'll be the bimbo beauty of the island.' They thought I was really delicate and afraid to get my hands dirty, but I just got stuck in there. Actually, I think I've surprised a few people already – a lot of people on that weekend didn't think I was capable of doing half the things that I did. Just goes to show, you can't judge a book by its cover, can you?

Vicki would prove that saying so true over her time on the island, although it has to be said that her chosen role model didn't exactly inspire confidence. 'I have a real thing about Barbie,' she admitted, "cos she can adapt to any situation. You can get Army Barbie, Ballet Barbie, and that's like me – I'll adapt to anything. I'm not just a bimbo, and I know for a fact that I'll stay the course. I've lived away from home for a while now, and I'm quite mature for my age. I've worked abroad as well. I'm just so determined to stay – I'll do it, even if it kills me.'

Just the right attitude, then, for the experience that awaited her. Also, and unlike many of the British castaways, Vicki had no real preconceived notions about what lay ahead. 'I hadn't really seen *Shipwrecked* before,' she explains, 'so I didn't really know what to expect. But once we got there, I have to admit I was just really shocked, and very worried [about] how we were going to cope. I have to say, I wasn't looking forward to it.'

Indeed, the first two weeks were very trying for her, and there were times when it was touch and go as to whether she'd stay or not. 'After a couple of weeks I said to myself, "Vick, you're kidding yourself if you think you're gonna last here for the whole ten weeks,"' she confesses. 'It just wasn't me – I need my nail files, I need my hair-straighteners; I can't cope on a bloody island.'

But, as we know, Barbie can adapt to anything, and Vicki soon pulled herself out of the dumps:

It got better after Gemma, Donna and Genevieve had left, because we really started working as a group then. In many ways, I thought that Donna and Gemma pulled each other down, while Sarah-Jane and me managed to lift each other up. I think they're really going to regret it when they see it on the TV and realized what they missed out on. But everyone noticed the change: in the beginning I didn't want to get my hands dirty; by the end of it I was like a bloody jungle woman, chopping down trees and stuff, and adapting to the situation. And that's when I really started enjoying it, and mixing more with the rest of the group. After that, I didn't think about leaving – it wasn't an option.

And if she needed to come up with one reason to be glad she stayed, Vicki can justifiably point to her nineteenth birthday on Yaukuvelevu. We've already established that birthdays were a much-needed boost to group morale and generally brought with them the promise of treats from The Goddess, but if you had to single out the wildest Yaukuvelevu party, then Day 26 was most assuredly it.

'I used to sleep on the beach most of the time, but the night before my birthday I just decided to sleep in one of the shelters,' she recalls, unaware that this simple but impromptu change in routine had already thrown a spanner in the works of the other castaways' plans:

I didn't realize till later, but that meant that the others had to sneak around the camp really quietly to make my surprise breakfast, but I slept through that until they all woke me up singing 'Happy Birthday'. And you know what? It was just beautiful. They'd made me a dish of fried yams – that was our favourite way of cooking them. And there was a whole papaya and coconut juice as well. And I know it might sound a bit silly to people who weren't out there, but it meant a lot. It took ages for papaya to ripen, so for them to give me a whole one was something else. And the gifts that they made were so special. I mean, back home, anyone can just walk into a shop and buy a present, but to walk along the beach collecting shells to make a necklace and so on was so much more special.

The Goddess didn't disappoint either, providing four bottles of rum, some boiled sweets and a packet of dried dates. And again, you can only begin to imagine how jaded the cast's palates were from their diet of yam and breadfruit, but all of them agreed that the dates tasted better than anything they'd eaten before. The rum? Well, we'll worry less about the flavour and point to the fact that this was Fijian rum, and 58 per cent proof. It was going to be quite a party, then.

Actually, the weather wasn't too good, but it really didn't matter – it was a fantastic birthday, and I'll never forget it. The thing about birthdays on the island, was that they really were about everyone and not just the person whose birthday it was. We'd get gifts from The Goddess, so there was something for everyone to share in. We had four bottles of Fijian rum, which is *really* strong. Just a couple of sips make you feel a bit giddy. So we were sat in a circle, passing these bottles around – each of us had to sing a line of a song, take a swig, then pass the bottle. And before I knew it, I was waking up thinking 'What's going on? When did I fall asleep?'. There were loads of bowls around me, so I knew that I'd been sick. Then I went off to HutCam with Randy, and I can't even remember what I was saying in there, I really can't. The next day everyone told me that I'd been playing on the bongos, singing and dancing, and it all started flashing back to me in little bits, and I was thinking, 'Ohhhhhh God.' It was a great party, and everyone really enjoyed it, but I think I got a little too drunk too quickly.

That much seems clear enough. We turn to Rainbow's diary for a slightly more lucid recollection of the night in question. 'As a group we're so much happier, nicer and fun when we've eaten well and had a bit to drink,' she wrote. 'And it's so lovely when Geordie plays guitar – it makes being here so much better.' At this point, the diary goes into capital letters with Rainbow announcing in no uncertain terms, 'I NEVER WANT TO SEE SALVO'S PENIS AGAIN!' Ah yes, our nudity-prone Sicilian Stripper had done his party piece once more, for the benefit of an audience who were by now plainly getting very used to it.

And it wasn't just the nudity that was beginning to bother Rainbow. When Vickj's system decided to reject the rum, Rainbow was on hand to help out. 'I held her head and Chloe-Jane held her waist while she puked into the bushes,' she wrote, 'and she just kept saying, "I'm so sorry, I'm really sorry."' But the thing that really upset me was after she passed out, Salvo started playing with her face, and then filmed her with CastCam. I said, "Leave her alone, she's ill," and he just said, "F**k off, I don't care".'

Vicki, plainly, was in no state to register any objections, but – despite some original misgivings about Salvo – was quick to stress that she found herself warming to him over the ten weeks. Back in England, just the mention of his name is enough to make her break into an ear-to-ear grin. 'I've spoken to Salvo quite a lot since I got back,' she laughs. 'I've actually got a message from him on my answerphone, saying, "Hello big breasts, hello beautiful breasts, I love you so much, you are the most beautifullest girl in the world and you've got the biggest breasts" – it's so funny! But he's really got to work on that chat-up technique, bless him.'

However, if Vicki warmed to Salvo, there's no question that her feelings for Leon were less amicable:

I actually really liked Leon to begin with, but as time went on, he really picked on me. Him and Salvo together, in fact, and both of them have a very strong personality, and found it very easy to influence the rest of the group. The boys *did* overpower the girls. Leon and Salvo picked on us because we were easy targets. Salvo would say stuff, and he really didn't realize how much he hurt people. I originally thought Leon was a really nice person, and actually quite attractive. But I came to hate him – everything he said irritated me, I couldn't stand to be with him, and my first impression just totally changed by the end. After a few weeks, I remember thinking 'How could I possibly have fancied him? He makes me feel physically sick!'

The heightened tension on the island also saw a very specific change in the usually docile Vicki. 'I'm not a very argumentative person,' she explains, 'but there were times out there that you just had to shout back at someone; you know, you're on an island, it's not like you can just storm off to your room and slam the door, you do have to have it out. And I'm actually really proud that I was able to do that on a few occasions.'

Having thrown the party of all parties, it's also worth noting that Vicki was involved in a few other wild nights on the island. First, there was the night of the 'Porno Cards':

Oh *God*... that happened on a day when we'd just received lots of sugar and coffee and our systems just weren't used to it – it kept us awake all night. And so, Sarah-Jane, Randy, Salvo and myself were sitting in a shelter, and Randy got out these playing cards. And he said, 'OK, Vicki, if I can guess the card you choose, you have to snog me'. He didn't guess it, but we went on playing like this, getting rid of cards along the way until there were only four cards left. And the forfeits were stuff like me having to kiss Randy for ten seconds, me having to kiss Sarah-Jane, having to flash your boobs and so on. We all swore a pact never to tell anyone about it, but the next day everyone knew, because Salvo had run around telling everyone he'd seen my nipples. He told *everybody.* Of course, me and Sarah-Jane were denying it all, while Salvo and Randy were exaggerating everything that happened as much as possible.

And if 'Porno Cards' wasn't enough, then how about 'Porno HutCam'? 'That was me and Sarah-Jane again,' giggles Vicki. 'We decided to do a special HutCam, with Sarah-Jane sitting on the bench with her boobs out, and me peeling off my bikini top, both of us giggling and playing up to the camera. It was just for a laugh,' she adds, 'but before long everyone in the camp knew all about our Porno HutCam – they just thought it was really funny, and the camera crew told us it wouldn't get used, which I was quite relieved about. My dad would go mad!'

It was on Vicki's birthday that Jeffro, like all the other castaways, wrote a little note in her diary, in which he said 'You're going to make your friends and family very proud of how you are coping here and I have every confidence that you'll be here to the very end. You're doing so well here, and you always look an absolute stunner.'

It was a far cry from the way Vicki had been perceived in the early days, and she was as aware as the rest of the castaways of the change that had taken place in her. 'When I first got to the island, I was very quiet within the group,' she admits:

I sort of kept myself to myself, when normally I'm actually very outgoing. I think I just wanted to know what everyone else was like before I showed my true self. And I admit that I *was* being very lazy in the beginning. I could have done a lot more work than I did. But after a few weeks of being upset and not feeling like doing anything, I started learning things, and wanting to do more. You know, you realize that it's a bit more important than just being in a TV programme, and you *have* to work to survive. I realized I was being selfish, and had to get off my backside and do something.

As if to confirm this, one of her proudest moments involved helping the group as a whole. 'One day, I suggested to Jeffro that we prayed to The Goddess,' she smiles. 'The next day, there was a note there saying "Your prayers will be answered in a matter of days, The Goddess is rising, so lift up your gaze." We were a bit confused by that, but we were happy that at least we'd been heard.' Two days later, on Day 41, the meaning of the riddle became clear when the sound of an aircraft engine was heard over the island. 'Everybody ran down to the beach, screaming,' recalls Vicki. 'There was a small plane circling the island, and I looked around and saw that every one of us was smiling – it felt great. The plane circled a few times, so we were just getting more and more excited, then it dropped two packages into the sea! I just screamed at the top of my voice – I can't explain the feelings [I was experiencing], but the grin on my face was so big!'

The airdrop had yielded a large bag of rice and some bottles of soy sauce – the kind of delivery that past *Shipwrecked* teams had taken for granted, but to this group, it was pretty much, well, a gift from the gods. As Vicki wrote in her diary, it also meant a change in her plans for the day. 'I'm so relieved,' she scribbled excitedly, 'Now we don't have to kill any chickens or dig up any ridiculously undergrown yams. I think today will be a day of relaxation and fun in the sun. And about time too!'

Back in England, Vicki was quick to point to the changes in attitude that the self-sufficiency had brought about:

Out there you had so much time to think, and you thought about all the things you take for granted most of the time. How you can just go to the fridge and grab something to eat, or just going to the shops for some bacon. Nobody will ever understand how hard it was – we had to kill a pig to get meat, we had to kill chickens... I mean, you go into a supermarket and buy a chicken breast without thinking about it, without it even occurring to you that something's had to die so you could have it. It made me realize how lucky we are – we've got it so easy, we really have. Before I went out I was always moaning that I was broke and feeling really hard done by; being on that island made me realize how ungrateful I'd been.

I couldn't wait to get back home, because I really missed my family. But I was amazed how hard it was adapting back to things. The first day I got back, my best mate came round and said, 'Come on, we've got to go out and see everybody,' so we went out and I was just shaking the whole time. We went to various bars and to a club, but I was terrified in a way – I hadn't seen so many people for so long, and it felt really claustrophobic, like I couldn't breathe. All these people were coming up and asking about the island, and I just couldn't handle it – I was just shaking to bits. And I felt so weird – usually I'd be the first person on the floor dancing, but I couldn't. Hearing all this garage music, instead of the bongos and the guitar. I just couldn't get back into it.

In her application letter to *Shipwrecked*, Vicki wrote: 'I want to be given this experience so that the little things in life would seem less important.' Ask her if that wish came true and she doesn't hesitate for a second. 'Completely true,' she smiles:

Before I went away I was out every night clubbing, but I've only been a few times since I got back. My friends have been saying 'You've gone different since you've been on

Shipwrecked, you never want to go out any more.' Fact is, I used to base my life around going out, I *had* to go out, *had* to get some clothes to go out in, but now it just doesn't seem as important any more. I've missed Yaukuvelevu so much, and I really didn't think I would. I'm so glad I went there – it made me a stronger person, and I proved a lot of people wrong by doing it. It's an experience never to be forgotten, and I'm so glad I got the chance to do it. You try telling people about it and it's so hard to cover the ten weeks in ten minutes, or even ten hours. So much happened out there. I'm sure there'll be bits of it still coming back to me in ten years' time.

And the hair straighteners? 'You know what? I didn't use them once. What a pointless thing to bring. I can't believe I ever brought them to the island,' she laughs. 'What *was* I thinking?'

11

LEON
EVANGELISTIS

Age: 25
Profession: Photography student/DJ
Luxury Item: *The Works of Homer*

It was Leon who perhaps most succinctly outlined the castaways' immediate predicament on their arrival at Yaukuvelevu, when he wrote in his diary:

> I think I should explain the circumstances we are in: we were all cast from three different parts of the world – Australia, USA and Britain. We all sort of knew something about the show, you know, deserted island for three months or so, food rations and so on. We've probably all seen the last show and all thought 'What a bunch of idiots! How hard can it be?'. Well I can tell you now, this show is *hard*. We have minimal clothes, no shelter materials like tarpaulin, and outside of a bottle of oil, some garlic and some salt and pepper, we have virtually NO rations. We were taught over two days on a neighbouring island the bare bones of survival methods: how to make traditional shelters and find food in the jungle, how to fish and use nets. We are hungry most days, some of us have lost

a lot of weight (myself included) and we are fatigued, but still alive.

One of the Australian contingent on the island, Leon rapidly became aware of some differences between him and his compatriots. 'I represent the ethnic majority of inner-city Australia,' he explained:

My background being second-generation Greek. Geordie's the direct contrast, and I love him to bits. I actually think Malia and myself were set up to clash personality-wise, but I think we surprised people by forming a bond. We're both outspoken, but it meant that we could thrash out our opinions and differences. She taught me something fantastic. She said worries are like little winds in your mind, and those winds will develop into tornadoes and gales if you don't open your mouth to express them. And I live by that now. Everyone needs a voice, otherwise you'll just go mental.

The one thing no one could accuse Leon is of not speaking his mind, although many felt that their ears were merely hearing him come up with a lot of well-chosen long words that ultimately had little substance to them. 'In a shipwrecked environment you have no choice of the people you end up with,' Leon reflected, 'and you can approach it in one of two ways: chill out and observe, or get involved and have your own say. I think my style is to have my say irrespective of what group of people I'm dealing with. Some find it arrogant, some say it's egotistical.'

A quick glance at Allan's diary entry for Day 6 confirms that last comment, this being the day that Leon – in the absence of any other candidates – was elected leader. As Allan wrote, 'He took the stage and set off on some psychological bulls**t trip – it was bog-roll sincerity that we would all wipe our arses on tomorrow. The meeting finished to a tumult of self-congratulatory back-slapping, with everyone saying, "Great meeting, guys." Embarrassing meeting, actually, guys – I won't abide the blowing of smoke up backsides anywhere, let alone in a small community like this.'

That view was confirmed by Jeffro: 'Leon came out with some crap, I can tell you. Sorry, but who does that bloke think he is? Dunno what it was about him, but he used all these long words in completely the wrong context, and I was like, "Leon, stop being so busy – you're making it hard for people." He seemed to want to be a leader the whole time. He was really hard to be around, actually, 'cos he was so negative about everything and everyone.'

That said, we're dealing with early impressions here, and as Chloe-Jane would confirm on her return to England, those kind of impressions were the last ones to trust:

At first I really didn't see eye to eye with Leon. We were like chalk and cheese and he opposed every idea I came up with, but towards the end we really bonded, spent a lot of time together and got on really well. I just really like [the fact] that you could get to know people so much better. No one really understood Leon – he was a very misunderstood person, tended to waffle a lot. But seeing through that, actually getting to what he meant to say, he was a really good person to have around, he just took a few too many words to get to what he was saying. Beneath all that he was a fantastic little character in his own right. And some of the stories he had were fantastic.

Leon can now add his part in the killing of the first pig to that list of stories. The subject of how animal slaughter was handled on the island became one of fierce debate, with many feeling that perhaps not enough respect was shown to the creature being sacrificed, but as a necessary evil, most accepted the unpleasantness. And it's clear from Leon's diary entry for that day that he didn't get as much pleasure from this as some had intimated:

> We killed a pig today. A little one, the female. I have a lot of respect for animals, and actually feel more compassion towards them than to some humans, and there are plenty of reasons as to why. Salvo elected himself to do the killing, so we climbed into the pen. The pig backed away in fear, and the larger one moved in to try to protect it – you could see the fear in their eyes. I reached towards the pig and it snapped at me – but I would do the same in its situation. It squealed, a really shrill noise, and then Salvo attacked with a recently sharpened blade, while three of us held the animal down. I could feel the last dying pulse reverberating against my knee. I noticed that some people backed away, some even left, but I'm sure they'll be very close when the pot's boiled and the meat is tender.

The instant bond between Salvo and Leon (Leon refers to him as 'My brother from another mother') was one that would endure for the whole of Leon's time on the island. 'I tell you,' he said on his return to Australia, 'if we hadn't had that wildman there to hurt himself on a daily basis, we'd have all been screwed. I'll tell you what, I think I've fallen in love with Salvo. His English improved so much,' he grins proudly, 'and that was because of my expert tutorials, of course. Nightly lessons that he forced me to give him when all I wanted to do was go to sleep – I had to go through his journal with him every night that I was on the island.'

And given that Salvo had never written English before, and had only a limited grasp of the spoken language, Leon was first to salute the man's achievement in writing two whole diaries. 'I would read his journal,' he recalls, 'and it struck me how magnificent it was, not only in its simplicity, but also in its honesty. I don't know how complex mine is, but I realized how well a point or expression is made when it's made simply. He wrote about certain people's selfishness, and his genuine feelings and aspirations for them to change their characters and become better people. I could not have done a better job of expressing my feelings.'

As the leader in Week 2, it fell to Leon to deal with the whole issue of Genevieve's behaviour. Aware that the manner in which the matter was dealt with might seem unduly harsh to an outsider, he's quick to defend the group's actions:

> Some people have some ingrained arrogance in their character, and even in the most extreme situations they just can't shrug it off. I saw that in Genevieve, and I formed that opinion of her straight away. Made it clear that I would rather not have to deal with her during the whole stay on the island, because of the insurrection she was causing. It was only going to get worse, and something had to be done – it was the best course of action, and I'm not apologetic about it.

Leon's opinions on the rest of the team are no less blunt. Some weeks later, and during the course of one of the less harmonious days, he would share his view of Rainbow: 'She gets to me on a lower level,' he wrote in his diary. 'Firstly, I think she is too filled with contradictions, is blatantly an exhibitionist with her feelings, yet somehow doesn't seem sincere. It looks to me like *she* believes what she says, but that's maybe something to do with being American, a struggling actress, and a hand-me-down hippy – to an Australian, that translates as "full of it".'

Not a man to mince his words, then. Leon spoke equally candidly about his disappointment with some members of the team when he returned to Melbourne:

> I'm not too much of a cynic, but I'm a bit wary of the way some people changed out there. You know, they started getting all happy and cheery, all 'let's work as a group', but in some ways it was still about presenting themselves a certain way, making themselves look better. And I'm sure there's another side to them as well. I was a lot older than the others. I had seven or eight years' experience on them, and it was like a different generation at times. I had real difficulty expressing myself on occasions, and probably ended up being really misunderstood.

That said, at least Leon and Salvo were attuned to each other. Indeed, in a weird moment of synchronicity, they even ended up sharing dreams. 'I dreamed last night,' wrote Leon in his diary, 'and not a good one. I'm concerned abut my family now, especially my father – I have to try and get in touch and find out if everything is OK. Then Salvo woke up next to me and announced he'd also had a bad dream; my face froze as he told me it had also been about his father. I'm concerned now. I'm more in tune with things in this place, where everything is stripped back – I take more notice and I listen more.'

Those fears, happily, proved unfounded, but another, more tangible problem soon began to make itself evident. Leon, by his very own admission, has an impossibly short attention span, and rarely lasts long in a job. And out on Yaukuvelevu, he was getting itchy feet for all kinds of reasons. On Day 38, his diary entry started out (and not for the first time) with the words 'Should I stay or should I go?' In a mixed emotional state, he shared his thoughts with fellow Australian, Geordie:

He doesn't like to approach a situation until it really needs it, but boy, did it need it. We talked by the net on the beach, got it all out and straightened out some confusion and perceptions about each other, but most importantly, I learned something. He told me to stick this out, that I would accomplish much more with this if I did. He thinks that I tend to quit things too easily in life, and he's right. He explained things very simply, and that was what I needed. I *will* finish this, or I will refuse to ever start anything else in my life.

And, of course, there were always reasons to stay on Yaukuvelevu – reasons you didn't have to look too hard to find. 'Who would have thought that I would be accepting coconut chunks from a naked Sicilian on a deserted Fijian island?' Leon wrote in his diary. 'That I would sunbathe naked on the beach next to said Sicilian, that I would be snorkelling nude amongst coral outcrops, surrounded by little fish? It's amazing.'

Leon's love for the island was not in question. The problem for him, unfortunately, seemed to be the people he was sharing it with. That, and an increasing annoyance with the fact that this experience was to be turned into a television programme, for the entertainment of people who, he felt, would never know what it was actually like out there. 'It's really important to me to have a sense of control over my destiny,' he admits, 'and I need that on a daily basis. Out there, they weren't giving you that freedom. It was like a real "us and them" thing. You might not understand the real psychological trauma of starving someone, but I do now – I've been there, and it's not a pretty set of circumstances. And I didn't want to be a puppet any more.'

Just a week before the end of the stay, Leon swallowed his earlier words about seeing it out, and decided to escape from Yaukuvelevu with the American, Randy:

It entailed a 4 kilometre ocean swim to the nearest inhab-
ited island, which is something I've never done before.
Randy came with me. The whole idea was just spurred on
by disappointment, really. And as far as escaping was
concerned, I've never been so committed to anything in my
life, and I could see the same in Randy's eyes. I've never
been in a war zone, but I can imagine people can react that
way in certain situations. I didn't care if I had a stroke or an
aneurysm on the way, I just wanted to get off that island.
That's how severe it was. The swim was really hard, and we
both got cramps and so on, but I never gave up – my mind
was strong. If you asked me to do it now, I'd probably sink
and die, but my mind then was just crazy – completely
loopy, man.

Looking back on it, he insists that he made the right decision:

By that time, I'd learned all I needed to learn, and all we had
to look forward to was another week of stupid arguments
that I had no patience with. That was the thing when people
upset you on the island. Back at home, you have the opportunity to just cross the road and never meet that person
again. Out there, you just had to bite your pride and let
things go at times. I think a lot of people used that tack
rather than being honest. And you've got to keep a level
of perspective about this. I mean, it's only a television
programme, but I saw in everyone's eyes while they were
on the island how they were going to get home full of mad
plans and how all this was going to change them. They
believed that totally, but I'm sure if I e-mailed them now I'd
find that they were just back in their usual existence and
pretty depressed about it all. I warned them about that.

As it transpired, Leon himself wouldn't find the return to civilization as smooth as he had anticipated: 'I ended up in Melbourne airport at about two in the morning with absolutely no cash on me, rang home and they refused to come and collect me! They're used to me like that, though – I've always been the kind of guy who goes off travelling at the drop of a hat and rolls back home broke as a joke at the end of it all, wanting a lift home.'

Once settled, though, he calmed down soon enough, and is quick to stress that the *Shipwrecked* experience was a valuable one for him. 'It was like a really intense version of normal life,' he grins. 'It was an amazing experience… I suppose my appreciation of things is a lot better, and it's given me a lot of determination, a real kick up the bum. My world's really opened up, and I'm good to go get the things I want now, but in a realistic fashion.'

Obviously, it remains to be seen whether Leon will eventually stick at one thing and manage to complete the tasks he sets himself, but it's to be hoped that his one regret isn't still top of his 'things to do' list. 'You know what, I'm just disappointed that I didn't kill everyone and eat them all!' he laughs. 'Why did I put up with that lot? I should've just killed them all! So yeah, that was a bit of a disappointment. But don't ever think that I didn't consider it. About, oh, fifty times a day at least in fact.'

12

SHAWN BOWEN

Age: 21
Profession: IT specialist/Airforce reserve
Luxury Item: Hammock (military issue)

It's a bit hard to know quite how to pigeonhole Shawn. On the one hand, you have a fierce patriot with a military background (as a US airforce reserve, he's served in Kosovo), a man who is prepared to die for his country. On the other hand, and going perhaps somewhat against the grain, you have the grade-A nutcase, a wildman serial-streaker, and an utterly unpredictable character boasting boundless reserves of energy when he chooses to use them. In short, for every stereotypical observation you can label him with, there's a wholly contradictory facet to his personality just waiting to catch you offguard.

It was the military training that first kicked in when Shawn learned he'd been selected to go on *Shipwrecked*. Having seen none of the show previously, he set about gathering intelligence from the internet. 'I've done quite a bit of investigating into *Shipwrecked*,' he confirmed before setting off, 'treated it like a mission. They always manage to screw up something, don't they? Pitch the camp somewhere where it'll get washed away, that kind of thing. Idiots. You won't get that out of me. But I looked at it and I thought, yep, this is perfect. It's not like *Survivor*, where you have to be mean all day long. I mean, we know there's going to be *some* problems...'

For Shawn, the first problem came when he received the standard issue *Shipwrecked* bag that would have to accommodate his worldly goods for the duration of the stay: 'Have you seen the size of it?' he laughed. 'You could fit a pair of socks in it! It's a bath-cap! I'm tempted to get a disposable camera, wrap it in plastic and shove it up my bum.'

Thankfully, no such emergency measures were required, and Shawn realized as soon as he reached the island that there were rather greater problems to be faced:

> The Brits had already been there for two days when we landed, and when we finally found them they showed us their camp – Geordie and me just looked at each other and you could see we were both thinking, 'Oh no, look at the state of this.' I mean there were pots, chopped-up logs and vitamin tablets all around the place, and I said, 'So where's the rice?' And they replied, 'No rice.' They said themselves that they didn't really have a clue what they were doing. I felt quite bad for them, but I was also quite disappointed with the lack of organization. But the look on their faces was like, 'Wow, we've been saved.'

Of course, you'd assume, and not unreasonably, that Shawn's training would immediately prove to be an asset on the island, although it rapidly emerged that theory, rather than actual practise was his speciality. By way of an example, Shawn's own website lists his skills as follows: 'Excellent presentation, facilitation and interpersonal skills. Demonstrated ability to work with diverse groups and all levels of an organization. Ability to communicate technical concepts to non-technical individuals. Training diverse background adults in areas of personal computing.' As Jeffro commented, 'Shawn's a funny one – he can talk and talk and talk. As long as it's about himself. I think he came on the island just to have a holiday. But I can't believe he kept it up all the way through, being so lazy. I would have been so conscious of people's respect for me, but obviously he didn't care, 'cos he did absolutely nothing.'

Indeed, when asked about his feelings about appearing on television, Shawn immediately joked:

TV show? What are you talking about? I went on vacation for a couple of months, I don't know anything about any TV show! Seriously though, being on TV was the least of my reasons for going out there. It was a once-in-a-lifetime opportunity, that's the real point. One thing that actually really irritated me out there was the fact that the Brits just seemed to be there to get their faces seen on TV, whereas the Australians and the Americans were more interested in actually living on an island. We wanted to go home and say we'd lived on an island, not that we'd been on a TV show. It sort of drew a line between the ten Brits and the six others.

That said, even Shawn's compatriots noted a certain reluctance on his part to leave his hammock during the early days. 'I'd just had a cold when I left,' he explained, 'and I hadn't told the producers anything about it, because if you're sick they won't let you go. I'd already lost 8 pounds the week before leaving and was completely out of energy – for the first week or so I just couldn't do anything. And the diet wasn't helping – it was eight days before I even used the Long Drop. Mind you, Allan went something like three weeks!'

Moreover, Shawn insisted that the work he put in went largely unnoticed, purely because he didn't actually bother drawing anybody's attention to it:

You could not know half the things that me and Geordie did. We'd go off on adventures and get stuff done, but everyone was still saying, 'Shawn never does anything.' The point was, I didn't call a camera crew each time I was going to do something. Allan was the worst for that in many ways – he'd announce that he was going to work in the garden for about an hour, and then he'd spend the rest of the day writing. But he kind of advertised the fact that he was working, whereas Geordie and me would just get on with things quietly.

Shawn would be the first to admit that the self-sufficiency aspect of Yaukuvelevu life didn't actually pose him many new challenges, but by way of compensation perhaps, he certainly had to deal with some of the dilemmas of communal living. Before setting off he announced a laid-back approach to arguments, pointing out that he didn't conflict with others easily. 'In those circumstances,' he explained, 'I just joke with people. If someone gets mad, I'll just joke about it. I don't get offended by people, I'm an adult.'

That kind of patience is admirable of course, but was tested to its full pretty much as soon as Shawn reached the island. On the first night the whole group spent together, a bit of alcohol-fuelled tomfoolery between Simon and Randy threatened to get out of hand, much to the concern of all the other castaways. Shawn, for his part, took at back seat to the main action. 'I tend to pull back from situations, sort of analyzing from a distance,' he explained. 'I guess that's just part of my military training. I was just sitting there watching the group from a distance, and when Randy and Simon started wrestling after a little too much rum, everyone was trying to separate them. I just thought "They're men – they can settle it." If two people want to fight, it's their choice – when it gets out of hand, *then* I'll step in.'

As he rightly predicted, there was no need for him to interfere at that particular moment, although that soon changed:

> Later on I went down to the beach to talk to Donna and Vicki, and Simon kicked a bit of sand in Vicki's face. I said 'Simon, do you mind? That's really not cool.' He was still drunk, and he just got completely out of hand, yelling and spitting in my face. Everyone was trying to pull him back, and I just lay there speaking very calmly. Not threatening him, just asking him to stop it. As far as I was concerned he was just drunk, and I didn't want to waste my time and energy on him – I needed to conserve my energy for the next ten weeks. I wasn't about to raise my pulse over it. Of course, the next day he was full of apologies and trying to make sure it didn't end up on camera, which was pretty stupid. I think that night was a turning point for him – after that he became two completely different people: there was 'Simon on-camera' and 'Simon off-camera'.

In fairness, Simon's behaviour on that night had troubled many of the group, although Shawn's concerns were more for Simon himself, rather than for the effect any of this might have on the team:

> He was so worried about that night. I guess he just didn't want his family to see him behaving like a drunken alcoholic – which he *is*, in my opinion, whether or not he admits to it. He speaks of all these stories about getting drunk and not knowing where he's woken up and he thinks it's really cool. I'd honestly like to think that when he got home he had a look at himself in that respect, but I gather that when he escaped to Dravuni on the ration run, he spent his time there just getting plastered. I mean, he's a really good guy –

when sober. I just wished he'd taken that opportunity to deal with his drinking.

It will come as no great surprise by now to hear that the next area of conflict involved a certain hot-headed Sicilian called Salvo. And, observing another *Shipwrecked* tradition, it involved nothing more important than a box of matches:

I was starting the fire to cook dinner, and the matches and the box were soaking wet, so the fire wouldn't light. When we eventually got it going I'd used around a dozen matches. Salvo noticed this and started going on, saying, 'Oh you stupid American, you don't know anything,' but I thought, 'Dude, I'm not going to bother with you right now.' He just kept insulting me, though. And I stress that I've never started a fight in my life, but it was like dealing with your kid brother – you knew that he wasn't going to shut up until you knocked him out. Eventually I started yelling back at him, and went off on one, insulting him. It was the first time anyone had jumped back at him and his face was like he'd seen a ghost. Then Allan jumped in and said, 'You know what, Salvo? We're sick of you doing this,' and calmed things down.

The second Salvo/Shawn flare-up occurred during their penultimate night on the island:

Me and Geordie had found some *huge* coconuts, and I was planning to give one of the shells to Geordie before leaving. So I was sat there skinning it and filing it down, when Salvo comes along and says, 'Oh, can I have that?' and I said, 'No, this is for Geordie', and again he starts going on about how I like Geordie more than I like him. Then he says, 'You want some of this? Come on down to the beach where there are no cameras and we sort it out.' Basically he wanted a fight, but for whatever reason he didn't want it to be on camera. So I started walking down, and by now I was honestly just *so* fed up with the guy – throughout the entire stay, he'd gotten into this habit of acting up and upsetting people, then five minutes later he'd apologize. It was just getting really tiresome, to a point where 'sorry' just didn't cut it any more. Anyway, he just sort of flicked my chest, so I grabbed his wrist and pulled him down to the ground. He said 'Oh, you want to fight? But I only tapped you!' and I just said, 'If you ever get close to me again, I'll break your wrists off'. And of course, five minutes later he comes over and apologizes.

Having promised to provide entertainment value on the island, Shawn felt that he was somehow becoming more and more subdued and not being his usual self. The others had noticed his quietness, but just assumed that was his normal demeanour. The turnabout came on 31 May, not in the shape of a kick up the back-side, but a kick in the face:

That day was a real turnaround for me. It was the day I was elected leader, and I was sitting there when the camera crew came up and said they were doing some filming around the theme of pain. At that stage, I was really sick of being down – I wasn't making people laugh like I normally do, and it was getting to me in a big way. I needed to do something off the wall. So I said to the soundman, 'Kick me in the jaw'. And you have to understand that I've always wanted to be a stunt man, so I'd studied all this stuff and knew what I was doing. So I'm sitting there, he kicks me, and just at the last moment I moved, but it looked like it connected. And that was it – I was back to normal. Next I ran into a tree, and the camera crew are like, 'Oh my god, what's happened to this kid?' I was just buzzing – it was like I'd had eight cokes. I had blood on my knees and elbows, and the crew couldn't believe it. But that's the kind of stuff I'm always doing back home with my mates.

The other highlight for Shawn (well, you have to improve on a kick in the face, after all) came, naturally enough, on the Fourth of July:

I almost left the island because of Independence Day. My whole family is very patriotic, it's inbred. And I'm willing to die for my country, no joke. So I just wanted to be home for the Fourth of July, because I've never *not* seen fireworks on that day. And no matter how hard we tried, we just couldn't get hold of fireworks for the island, no way, no how. So I was trying to stuff lighter fuel into a bamboo stick, with papaya seeds and coals, and me and Geordie had planned on building a huge catapult so we could launch burning logs from it, just trying anything we could to make things look like fireworks.

As it turned out, amateur pyrotechnics would not be required on the day, which started out with a delivery from The Goddess: picnic goodies, rice, flour, beer and, of course, good old American apple pie. 'The day was awesome,' grins Shawn:

Everyone wished America a happy birthday, and I was really pleased about that, you know, that people actually respected the day for what it was. And The Goddess had left an American flag in my and Geordie's favourite spot, which was the best feeling ever. And it was a *good* flag, you know, embroidered, each stripe sewn individually. I looked closer and saw the label 'US Government Issue' and just thought, 'Hmmm, how on *earth* did they get this?' Turned out they'd borrowed it from the US embassy on Fiji! But what was *really* cool was that Malia, Chloe-Jane and Jeffro did their own 'human firework' display — Malia was a Catherine Wheel, Jeffro was J'ro Rocket and Chloe-Jane was CJ Banger. It just made me feel awesome that they all really understood what the day meant to me.

Well, *nearly* all of them... as Allan recalls, 'for the rest of us, Independence Day was like, "Great, loads of food." Shawn, on the other hand, put up the American flag, looked at it and said, "Oh my god, that's the most beautiful thing I've ever seen." A flag?!' Allan chuckles in disbelief, but is quick to confirm that Shawn made quite an impression on him over the time they spent together:

To be perfectly honest, I've no idea what Shawn was out there for. He actually said he was there for his country at one point, which we thought was hilarious. I'll be honest, at the beginning I couldn't stand him. I remember asking him, 'So what's your story, then?' and he said, 'I only answer direct questions.' Two weeks later, you couldn't shut him up! He'd gone through his entire history at least three times. Jeffro once asked him what the big deal with prom dances was. Half an hour later, we knew exactly how many games there were in a college football season, but we still hadn't heard a word about proms. He'll talk the hind legs off a donkey, that guy. But once you'd spent time with him, gotten to know him and let him get to know you, he was a real diamond bloke, the kind of guy who'd run through a brick wall for you.

Allan also rather neatly described Shawn as 'Someone who looks calm, but also looks like he could hurt you.' Shawn pronounced himself delighted with the description, but suggested just the one alteration: 'I just told him all he needed to add was "...and *would*"' he laughs.

Back in America, Shawn remarked that the island experience had arguably had less of an impact on him than on others. 'In some ways the atmosphere out there was very new to me,' he concedes, 'but a lot of the stuff we did I was already familiar with. It made me realize that people who seem outwardly incompetent aren't necessarily going to stay that way. Sarah-Jane and Vicki really changed, and I'm very proud of them. Actually, I'd say Sarah-Jane probably gained the most from it on a personal level. As far as what *I* got out of it, well, Geordie is someone I'd hope to stay in touch with for the rest of my life. And if you come out of it with a friend like that, you've nothing to complain about, really.'

And by way of final confirmation that normal service had been resumed? 'I don't think it changed me at all,' he chuckles. 'When I got home I was right back to being my usual self: the first thing I did was run around the block naked!'

13

DONNA
JOHNSON

Age: 19
Profession: Barmaid/'Skivvy'
Luxury Item: Tobacco

While you've already read about the selection process, the gruelling weekend of team exercises that all the castaways experienced before being chosen for the programme, it should be pointed out that one of the team found a rather simpler passage to Yaukuvelevu. Nineteen-year-old Donna Johnson from Blackpool came across a reader's competition to become a TV castaway in an issue of *heat* magazine and found herself unable to resist.

'I actually saw the competition while I was watching an episode of *Shipwrecked*,' she recalls, 'and I just thought, right, I'll go in for it. I mean, all you had to do to start with was name the island they went to in the last series of *Shipwrecked*. I didn't tell anyone I'd entered, and I soon forgot about it myself, to be honest, because I never win anything. Then I got a phone call saying I was one of the names pulled out of the hat, and they asked me to go in to T4 for the final selection.' And it was on Channel 4's T4 weekend programme that Donna found herself in front of the cameras well before any of the other castaways. 'All we had to do was build a sandcastle,' she explains, 'and then there was a viewers' phone-in poll on, which was the best, and that was it, Bob's your uncle! I couldn't believe it!' she laughs. 'Who'd have thought it?'

Donna was perfectly clear about her reasons for wanting to be Shipwrecked before she went out to the island. 'I've always wanted to do something in theatre or telly,' she admits, 'but I was never sure which way to go about it.' However, there is one major potential stumbling block in that particular career plan, namely the fact that Donna, by her own admission, has no theatrical talent. Not that she's about to let this stop her achieving her dreams. 'I can't sing,' she laughs, 'I've got two left feet and my arse takes control when I dance. So I think I'll make a really good TV presenter. I've always wanted to be famous, and I'm not bothered how I get there. Just like Geri Halliwell, really.' Er, Geri Halliwell? 'Yes!' insists Donna, 'She's my absolute idol – I think she's fantastic.'

Like many of the other castaways, Donna was quite convinced that she was made of the right stuff for the demands of island survival, but – again, like many of them – she was also labouring under the misapprehension that this series would be just like the preceding ones. In fact, it could be argued that this particular aspect of the stay would, in time, affect her more keenly than the rest.

Asked before setting out if she had any concerns about living rough, she replied:

Well you don't get toilet paper, do you? I know there'll be a hole in the floor, and I'm not bothered about that – I've peed in worse places, I can tell you! And I know I can live without make-up, but I'm addicted to shopping, so I'm really going to miss that. Still, it's all about the experience, isn't it? You can't knock that back, just because you're worried you're going to miss your family and friends. My sister was actually going to get me a card saying 'Stick it out' and then she decided not to – she thought it sounded like she didn't have faith in me. I told her, 'You don't need to have faith in me – this is my big chance, and I'm not going to blow it.' You don't look a gift-horse in the mouth, do you, so I'm just going to grab this gift-horse and throw it round my shoulder and get on with it. I just can't bloody wait. There aren't words in the dictionary to explain how I feel.

On the subject of missing out on three home-cooked meals a day, she simply laughed: 'I dunno about that – we might starve and turn into cannibals!'

Having made the final team via a very different route, though, Donna, from the very beginning, lacked the communal confidence that the others had already begun to experience at the selection weekend. 'I don't know a thing about any of the others,' she admitted, 'and I'm really nervous about that.' Her arrival at the airport confirmed those fears:

I felt like a total outsider from the start. As soon as I got to the airport the programme-makers hid me upstairs in a café out of the way, so that they could surprise the others. I was the only person whom no one knew, whereas all the others knew each other already. I was so nervous when the crew finally brought me downstairs. There was a camera crew, this huge light shining in my face, and about 30 or 40 people waiting! Right then, I just wanted the ground to swallow me up – it was the worst feeling ever. But they were really nice, really welcoming. I clicked with Gemma straight away, but they were all absolutely lovely.

With those initial fears laid to rest, Donna flew off to Fiji with the others, and it's here that her diary reveals the next problem that she faced. On arrival at Fiji she wrote, 'After such a long flight, we went straight to the hotel to get ourselves some breakfast – toast, croissants, fruit and cereal – and I made sure I got my money's worth, because we're going to be living off nothing but rice and cabbage for the next ten weeks.' Plainly, this was not to be the case, but there was also another teensy snag on the horizon, namely that Donna, as she freely confirms, is not the easiest person to feed. Recalling the pre-island training that the castaways all received on the neighbouring island of Dravuni, she chuckles: 'For a couple of hours a day, they'd walk us round Dravuni, pointing out what we could eat and how we should cook it, and I was just thinking "That looks minging, I'm not going to eat *that*." Then we went fishing for an hour, and managed to catch one fish, the size of your little finger, between us. It wouldn't have fed anyone!'

As she confirms, the real nature of the island experience was still not fully known, but the truth was slowly beginning to dawn on the group. 'I still honestly thought we were going to get cabbage and rice,' she admits, 'and even when we were told that it was going to be hardcore, we still thought, "Yeah, we can hack it, no probs". They said, "No, *really*, you don't understand: you're going to get no help, it's going to be ten weeks of hardcore survival." I just thought, "Oh my God, what have I let myself in for here?"'

If worries had started to surface in Donna's mind at that moment, they were quickly dispelled on arrival at the island of Yaukuvelevu itself:

When we actually got there, we ran around the island like headless chickens – which is an unfortunate choice of expression given what was to come. We set about exploring it in teams of two, and it really was absolutely beautiful. So *huge*. From a distance it just looked like a massive heap of forest, but as soon as we got there and saw all these

Sarah, Gemma, Donna and Vicki often considered spitting in Salvo's dinner.

There were never enough chairs at the table.

⊕

Leon was a big hit with the laydees...

Vicki, CJ and Sarah-Jane tried not to laugh at Simon's new hairdo.

⊕

⊕

'Deceptively spacious pied-a-terre, would suit first-time buyer...'

Sleeping on the beach was positively encouraged.

⊕

On special occasions, Salvo would actually wear clothes.

Clubbing, Yaukuvelevu-style: Geordie on guitar, Rainbow on drums.

Malia didn't know the words to 'Bob the Builder', but struggled valiantly anyway.

⊕
Geordie's Jamiroquai obsession was
beginning to worry the others.

Malia was so proud of Jeffro's progress
in her 'Gender Studies' classes...
⊕

⊕

Moles had apparently attacked the beach during the night.

The garden was in need of some attention, it seemed...

⊕

Allan would while away the quieter days whitewashing the trees.

Leon won the 'showbiz grin' competition.

'Please do not feed the animals.'

beaches, oh it was *gorgeous*. Especially when you went to the highest point of the island and you could see for absolutely miles. It was really like an advert, palm trees dipping into the ocean, absolutely beautiful.

As one of the 'British girls' contingent who would go on to set up their own separate group, Donna, like all the others, felt that the treatment Genevieve received was at best unfair, although she also sheds a little light on the niggling problems that lay behind the actual accusations, namely the fact that Genevieve made it very difficult for people to trust her:

> As far as the separate girls' camp went, we were a bit serious about it, I suppose, but it was mostly a bit of fun – you know, spice up the programme a bit, 'cos we were just getting really bored and there was all that two-facedness going on about Genevieve, which was really getting us down. Mind you, Genevieve was very devious – she kept things quiet. We all had our luxury items, and both me and Genevieve had chosen tobacco. Now, I used to share mine out with anyone who smoked, but Genevieve used to always say that she didn't have any left. So I gave her a fair bit of mine, but I later found out that she had hers stashed away and would go into the bushes in secret and smoke it on her own. So she was devious that way, but she was a really lovely girl as well, and I just think that they were really unfair to her.

Like Vicki, Sarah-Jane and Gemma, Donna had originally said that she would leave the island if Genevieve was expelled. It was a pact the girls had made when the group originally announced their intention of putting Genevieve to the vote, although they were all persuaded to stay, partly by the group appealing to them, partly by

Genevieve's insistence that they stick it out. That said, Donna was still finding the experience very wearing, and shortly after Genevieve's departure, her doubts found their way into her diary. 'I'm thinking of escaping from the island,' she wrote. 'I know people are going to think I'm totally and utterly crazy and completely off my trolley, but the way I see it, I'll get to eat decent food, be able to go to the toilet without a swarm of flies buzzing around me, sleep in a proper bed, but most of all, I'll get to see my mum.'

The rest of the castaways were obviously aware that Donna was far from happy, but few of them knew the real reasons for it. Indeed, Donna made a point of keeping her worries private, to the point of not even mentioning them in her diary. It was only when she'd returned to England that she explained what had been going through her mind:

> Around the second week, I just got a really strong gut feel-
> ing that something was wrong with my mum back at home.
> To start with, I just thought 'ignore it'. I'd never been away
> from my mum for so long without any way of contacting
> her, so it was only natural that I'd be worried. But when I
> did get home in June, I found that there had been something
> wrong back at home – that was all a bit spooky. And I didn't
> write about it or talk about it because it was just something
> private, but people could see how upset I was, even if they
> didn't know why.

Added to the worries back home, there was one particular problem on the island for Donna. And it'll come as little surprise by
now to learn that that problem was Salvo:

> When I first met him, he seemed really, really nice. And he
> was really funny on the plane. But then he just kept saying

and doing the same things over and over again, till they just weren't funny any more. To be honest, I just couldn't stand him – he did my head in. He kept asking everyone for their phone numbers so we would stay in touch when we got home, but I refused to give him mine. And then there was 'The Salvo Show'! Every bloody day he'd be in HutCam doing that, and it got so boring. He kept asking me to go into HutCam with him, but I just said no.

In fairness, and like most of the others, Donna was quick to point out the Sicilian's good points. But unfortunately, it was when Salvo fell sick that, for Donna and for many of the other castaways, he was at his best. 'When he was ill, he was OK,' she laughs, 'because he'd go really quiet for a while, and that was *such* a relief. But then he'd get better, and for the rest of us, that basically meant he got worse.'

Salvo may not have been the only reason that Donna and Gemma decided to leave, but it's generally agreed that he had a part to play in the fact that they were less than happy on Yaukuvelevu. On one occasion, Salvo had killed two chickens for dinner, and the girls made the diplomatic faux-pas of asking not him, but Geordie about the correct way to pluck and gut the birds. As Donna wrote in her diary, 'Salvo wasn't at all happy about that, since he wanted to give his opinion, as usual, so he decided to take it out on me, calling me fat and saying I had a huge arse. I completely snapped. I tried so hard not to rise to the bait, but I'm sick to death of people calling me fat! I know I'm the biggest girl here, but is there any need to be so shallow and start making comments about it?'

That aside, Donna proved herself more than capable of giving as good as she gets when she came to discuss Salvo's own physical shortcomings. 'He thought he was God's gift to women, but he wasn't well blessed, if you know what I mean,' she chuckled. 'I was amazed when he kept going on about how many women he'd slept with – I just thought, "Mate, you could never satisfy *anyone* with that." Chloe-Jane once asked me if I minded Salvo being naked all the time, and I said, "No, it's not like you can see owt."'

But the clash of personalities, combined with the threadbare food situation, was slowly taking its toll. As Donna wrote in her diary, 'I need to leave this place – I just can't be myself here. Don't get me wrong, there are some wicked people here, but there are also some not-so-wicked people and they're the ones who put you on downers. Recently, all I seem to write are negative thoughts, but anyone who was here would understand that completely.'

A few of the others ventured the opinion that Donna's problems partly stemmed from the fact that she was suffering nicotine withdrawal symptoms, although they didn't realize that the canny Blackpool lass had found an outside source of tobacco. 'Some of the local fishermen started sneaking me fags,' she admitted, 'which was well weird after you're used to smoking roll-ups. They gave me a Marlboro light and it was like smoking a big fat cigar. I smoked it halfway down the filter – had to get as much value out of it as possible!'

The nicotine highs were not enough, though, and after having explored various possible escape avenues, Gemma and Donna finally asked the group to vote them off the island. The two girls each made a speech to the rest of the group explaining why they wanted to leave, and despite much encouragement and persuasion from the disappointed castaways, they remained firm in their decision to bail out of the experience. It was with considerable reluctance, then, that the group eventually allowed them their wish.

Donna's last night on the island was a sleep-free affair, as she wrote in her diary:

I was just so excited, knowing that I was going home. It felt weird, but great. There were several times when I woke up in the night, but one particular one that I remember was opening my eyes, looking up at the sky and thinking about home and about Mum. And then I saw a gold star right above me – I didn't believe it at first, but Gemma saw it as well, and it was beautiful – like nothing I've ever seen before. I suddenly remembered something my mum had told me. 'When you look up at the stars, just remember, those are the same stars I'll be looking at back at home.' Suddenly the gold star seemed like a symbol, one of me being happy at last.

The next morning, the boat arrived to return the two girls to Dravuni:

I got up, having had no sleep at all, got into my scruffy clothes, brushed my teeth in the sea for the very last time and just looked forward to no more sleeping on the beach, no more eating yams, no more dodgy stomachs, no more running to the Long Drop in the middle of the night. We said our goodbyes, and everyone was crying except me. I just couldn't. I was laughing my head off, to be honest. I was so happy. On top of the world, I was. Just didn't care, because I was going home. Malia made me cry when we left. She had tears in her eyes and pulled me to one side and said, 'Please don't go – I really don't want you to leave.' She's so lovely, Malia. Really down to earth.

And it's only fitting that the girl who referred to pretty much every island meal as being 'minging' should arrive on the next island and immediately start talking about food. 'When we got to

Dravuni, me and Gemma just ate like we'd never eaten before: eight slices of toast, then a peanut-butter-and-jam sandwich – which is minging, by the way, don't try it – then we had a very large Big Mac Meal with Chicken McNuggets, cheeseburger and chips and everything. And yes,' she laughs. 'It all came up the way it went in – our systems couldn't cope with it.'

Back in Blackpool, Donna is perfectly candid about her experience as a TV castaway, and the way she thinks she'll be perceived by the viewers:

I probably did come across as being lazy, but honestly, I'm really not like that – I just needed an energy boost. I also think that everyone was very conscious about how they were going to come across on TV – you find yourself having to think before you speak, and I'm not used to doing that. Everyone, in the back of their minds, was thinking about the TV side of things, but when you get out of there and realize the amount of effort you've put in for your five minutes of fame, it's just not worth it at all. I was so determined to be famous, but it got to a point where it wasn't worth dying for, and I just thought, 'Sod it, go back home and become famous somehow else.'

Coming home was really mental. It was really weird seeing people again! But Gemma and I were both absolutely glowing and so happy when we got off the plane. All I wanted then was a nice cup of tea and a fag. As soon as I got back to Blackpool, my mates keep saying, 'Why did you come back?' and I tell them I wasn't happy there, and they're all saying 'Well I could have done it,' but the fact is, they couldn't. They couldn't last an hour without a hairbrush or a mirror! When it comes on TV, I still don't think they're going to realize how hard it was.

Strangely, for one whose aspirations were to follow in the high-profile footsteps of Ginger Spice, Donna is now actually less then thrilled about the prospect of seeing herself on television. 'When the programme comes on telly, I'm leaving Blackpool,' she laughs. 'I mean, me on telly in a bikini? Hello beached whale of Blackpool! All my mates are just going to let rip completely. I'm working in a pub in Blackpool and they're threatening to put it on the widescreen TV when it comes on, so I won't tell them when it's starting.' Donna also jokingly points to the 'Yaukuvelevu Make-over' effect. 'When I came home,' she smiles, 'I had a lovely flat stomach – but that's gone already. I've got more rolls than a bakery now! Dreadful! And I've still got scars all over my legs where I was bitten by sandmites. They were hideous. It looks like I've had measles or something!'

If it's starting to sound like Donna regrets her time on the island, she's very quick to put us straight:

Don't get me wrong, I *did* enjoy it there. I was very happy to have been given the chance to do this, but there really was nothing to do and I just got more and more depressed. After I got back, I used to find myself wondering what the others were doing now on the island, but I never wanted to be back there with them. It actually feels like a dream, like it never happened.

And as for the next move? 'Let's put it this way,' she chuckles, 'I will *never* enter a competition in my life again!'

14

PIERRE HUGUENY
(MAN FRIDAY)

Age: 21

Profession: Film student

Luxury Item: Lots of food for the other
   castaways!

Odd bunch, these French contestants. One leaves just two weeks into the *Shipwrecked* saga, and then another one arrives three weeks before the end of it. Although it could be fairly argued that Genevieve had some control over her fate in that regard, there was no such luxury for Pierre who – despite having been chosen at the selection weekend – wasn't entirely sure if he would even make it to Yaukuvelevu.

A keen rugby player, Pierre arrived at the selection camp already wounded. As he explains, 'The weekend before, I'd injured my knee in a rugby game. I did a serious tackle on another player, the best tackle I'd ever done, and when I hit the ground I twisted my knee. But it *was* a great tackle – my very best.' Starting out on the wrong foot, so to speak, Pierre found it difficult to enjoy that whole weekend. 'I couldn't join in with the activities, and I ended up helping the staff, cleaning floors and preparing meals,' he recalls, 'so my motivation was missing, really.'

Still, he endeavoured to make the best of the situation,

although increasingly it began to appear as though nothing would go in his favour:

> On the Friday evening I met a girl called Aiko, and I really liked her. But then she dropped out of the selection weekend, which really upset me — I was so depressed, and to be honest I felt like giving up as well. I just couldn't be bothered any more. And every time I started getting on with someone else, they were dropped from the group. Every single time! But on the Saturday night we went into the woods, you know, camping and killing rabbits, and it started getting exciting. I found my motivation then.

Pierre certainly impressed the selection panel, although his knee injury presented them with a problem and it became clear that a contingency plan was required. 'When I was selected, they still didn't know if my leg would be OK,' explains Pierre, 'so they told Simon that if I wasn't fit, then he'd be going in my place.' It was this substitution that would lead to Simon referring to himself as 'the reject', although he was the only one to even think of it in those terms.

For Pierre, the final word on his progress came about a week and a half before the castaways were due to fly out to the South Pacific:

> I had to have a small operation to remove some cartilage from my knee, and when I woke up, the doctor told me that there was absolutely no way I could go. I was so depressed. I just went home, and lay on the sofa recuperating. I really had no motivation at all. Basically, everything I'd done since Christmas had been geared around going on *Shipwrecked*, so when I'd been told I couldn't go, that was it for me — it was all over.

But even if it seemed as though he'd missed out on the opportunity to be there himself, Pierre still wanted to follow the group's progress on Yaukuvelevu. 'I would phone the RDF offices about four times a week to find out how they were getting on,' he admits. 'I didn't quite know how, but I still really wanted to be a part of it, and was so upset not to be there.'

Those weeks were, as Pierre would later comment, a miserable time for him. Having spent the best part of half a year dreaming about the *Shipwrecked* programme, having managed to get through all the selection processes, he just seemed to keep hitting one obstacle after another. But even the faintest hope of getting a chance to go out to Yaukuvelevu was enough to convince him to stay at his student home in Hartlepool, rather than returning to his family's house in Strasbourg.

A few weeks after the knee operation, though, a phone call from the *Shipwrecked* production crew in Fiji offered a very real sign of hope:

They rang me and said that there was maybe a way for me to join the others on the island. They explained the idea of Man Friday, and I was really enthusiastic about it. Even then, though, it still wasn't definite, so I had to keep reminding myself that it might not happen, but I was very excited all the same. From that day on, my bag was all packed and ready. Then, in mid-May, they phoned me again and explained that I had to come to London the next day. I was so thrilled − I'd had nothing to do for over a month, and hadn't really been in the mood to go out or meet up with friends. It was a wonderful feeling to know that I was going. I'd been so excited when I passed the selection weekend in the first place, but this was twice as wonderful.

There remained, however, the matter of the injury. 'They needed a note from my doctor saying that I was fit to fly,' explained Pierre, 'and in truth, my knee still wasn't really OK, but I asked my doctor to give me the all-clear, and because he's a really nice guy, he did. I just had the hugest smile on my face. And the hospital staff were really happy for me as well.' If fate hadn't smiled on Pierre before that point, it was certainly giving him a friendly wink now, and after so many false starts he was finally on his way to Yaukuvelevu.

The castaways had no idea who 'Man Friday' actually was. All they had been told was that they had a lifeline – if times got too hard, then they could summon him or her, and they would receive what they needed at that given time. And the timing was key, it soon transpired. The island's yam supplies were wearing thin, the supplies of rice that had recently been air-dropped were all but gone, and the old camp catchphrase of 'I'm hungry!' had returned to punctuate every conversation.

By the time Day 44 dawned, the castaways had few nutritional resources left and as Chloe-Jane wrote in her diary, 'What happened next could not have been better timed! We were all having breakfast, when some of the group ran up from the beach and said they'd seen a large boat approaching. It could only mean one thing: MAN FRIDAY! We all gathered on the beach to watch the boat drawing near – I looked through the binoculars, and all I could make out was the outline of one person surrounded by palm leaves that had been used to decorate the boat.' Chloe-Jane had, in fact, requested a special delivery from Man Friday in the form of her boyfriend from back home, Ian. 'As the boat came closer,' she continued, 'I could make out a tall white guy with dark hair, and for one split-second I really thought it was Ian. For that instant I was euphoric!'

Her disappointment at realizing that it was Pierre rather than Ian was, however, very short-lived. 'I ran into the sea and gave Pierre a huge, huge hug. I was ecstatic to see him, as we'd gotten on so well at the selection weekend.' For Pierre, the sight of all these faces beaming at him was the best reception he could have wished for. 'Getting to the island was amazing,' he chuckles. 'It was something I'd waited for for such a long time, and the first people I saw were Allan and Chloe-Jane. I was really pleased to see them. I realized quite quickly that Genevieve was no longer there, but I was surprised to see the Australians and Americans.'

But the sheer joy of having a new face on the island was also tempered by an awareness that the dynamics of the established community would now be required to adapt to include a newcomer, one who provided the castaways with a much-needed link to the world that they'd left behind, as Pierre recalls:

> It was weird. Everyone had so much to tell me about what had happened on the island, and they also wanted to know all about what had been going on back at home. There was so much information to take in. They wanted to know who was number one in the charts, what was on at the cinema, silly stuff like that. But it gave them something new and different to talk about, instead of talking about each other. I soon realized that on the island, without access to outside information, the only thing to talk about was the other castaways, which just made the atmosphere bad.

Understandably, the newest member of the family had anxieties of his own regarding the need to adapt to a whole new way of life. 'I was really scared when I arrived,' admits Pierre, 'and for all kinds of reasons. Firstly, since I was joining halfway through, I knew people would judge me, and not necessarily in a good way. I think some of them felt that I wasn't a true survivor, but it's not as though that was my fault. Also, I'm not very confident about speaking English, so that worried me too. I can't really explain, but it was just very scary.'

In an attempt to show Pierre that he was truly welcome, the group proceeded to elect him leader. However, while touched by the gesture, he also couldn't help feeling that it was 'just a little bit stupid':

Actually, Andi Peters asked me at the selection weekend if I wanted to be leader and I explained that I didn't. I'm just not interested in that, and I don't really see myself as the right person to control a group. They made me leader to show that they were pleased I was there, and that they accepted me. But I was new on the island, and I didn't really understand their rules, or know about the arguments and debates that had happened before. In some ways, maybe that was actually a positive thing – it meant that I had a new approach. If they'd made me leader a few weeks later, I'd have been approaching it in the same way as everyone else.

Immediately, an underlying current of tension became apparent, one that was neatly explained by Allan:

It was quite a problem, Pierre arriving when he did. I mean, it was brilliant to see him, and he was the best possible person that they could have picked, but the rest of us had already settled into a routine by then, one that we knew off by heart and that we understood. And it sounds odd, but it only takes one person being added to the team to disrupt that pattern. His way of doing things was different, and because of the language barrier he had a way of saying things that grated with people who'd been doing this for nigh-on two months. He wanted the whole experience, and there was sadly no way he'd get it in just three weeks. But he got everything he could out of it.

Pierre's first diplomatic faux-pas happened the very next day at breakfast. He sat down to the castaways' favourite breakfast of rice-pudding made with coconut milk and immediately pronounced it 'the worst breakfast I have ever eaten in my life'. As Chloe-Jane observed, 'Pierre has no idea what it's like to eat breadfruit with brown water as your main meal, what it's like to dig out yams on a steep, slippery slope, with cockroaches and ants crawling up your arms and legs, NO IDEA AT ALL!' As Allan pointed out, though, 'Pierre had put loads of soy sauce into his — too much by far. So it probably *did* taste revolting. But his comment went down pretty badly with everyone there.'

Before long, Jeffro would also note the need for both sides to adapt to the newcomer. 'Me and Chloe took Pierre on a tour of the island,' he grins, 'and when we came to the yam patch, we said, "Right, this is where you have to get your hands dirty and start digging." And he said, "Oh no, I am not the keen gardener, I want to go scuba-diving." Me and Chloe just cracked up, but I tell you, if Leon and Salvo had been there, they'd have killed him! Bless him, he'd just arrived, fresh from civilization, and he just didn't realize. He had to adapt, but at the same time we had to adapt to him.'

In fairness, Pierre hadn't had to experience some of the harsher times on the island and had little understanding of just how drained of energy his friends had been. Arriving there full of energy, he was dismayed to see how little they'd achieved. 'I was a little disappointed that people did so little,' he would later admit. 'We were on the island to learn, and some people came away having learned absolutely nothing. I was astonished to find that some people hadn't even explored the whole island! It's a bit like buying a new house and never using the top floor.'

As the days went on, Pierre gained more and more insights into the workings of the community and — once more — was less than impressed by what he observed:

Different people joined the project for different reasons. Some, like myself, were there for the experience. In fact, I probably would have enjoyed it more if there hadn't been any cameras there. Some others were more ambitious, and were there to have a holiday and be seen on camera. Because of that, we didn't truly function as a team. There were people there who didn't even know where the cooking or gardening equipment was! And I think that people like Leon just wanted to create conflict. He would do anything to be the centre of attention.

Leon's departure from Yaukuvelevu was, in fact, one of the highlights of Pierre's time there ('I know that sounds bad,' he frowns, 'but it's true'), although he was rather less pleased when Simon, the castaway who'd been given Pierre's place on the island, decided to make an early exit after the ration run. In his diary, Pierre wrote to Simon, explaining his feelings about this. 'I'm upset and pissed off,' he wrote. 'You need to know that I'm offended because you had my place here, and I think you should have stayed, if only out of respect. I think some of the people here are acting, pretending to be sad in front of the camera, then playing cards and having fun when the cameras go. It's hypocritical and selfish. Actually, come to think of it, when I look at that kind of behaviour, maybe you did make the right choice.'

Of course, it would be unfair to give the impression that Pierre had been totally disappointed by what he discovered on the island; indeed, there were definite signs that his short-lived interest in Aiko on the selection weekend had all but been discarded in favour of a new flame...

Ah, yes, I really, really liked Malia, she was my favourite girl there. I promised her that within the next five years I'll go out to Australia to see her. At the moment I'm working a lot, so hopefully I can go and see her next summer. It's all I think about at the moment. I've been working fifteen hours a day without a break to get the money together. I tell you, I love Malia.

Looking back over the whole of his — admittedly brief — experience of life as a castaway, Pierre has no doubt about whose company he enjoyed the most:

The people I liked most were the Fijians. Honestly — they're great people. When we left the island, I had the best party of my life with them. When we left Yaukuvelevu for Dravuni, the other castaways were only interested in sleeping and eating. And when we got to Suva island, some of them spent the whole afternoon in McDonald's, rather than actually exploring the place! I went off to the market, found all the little shops and stalls where the tourists don't go, and in the afternoon I went to a nightclub where I was the only white person — it was magical. The Fijians were so natural. I never cry, but when I left Fiji I was very close to tears.

Pierre would be the first to admit that he came away from the experience with a far greater faith in fate — having seen an experience taken away from him, only for it to return quite unexpectedly has given him a whole new perspective on how luck can treat an individual. And as far as living on a desert island goes? 'Well, I think I can survive well now,' he shrugs. 'But I don't think I can survive in a group. If I was asked to go on the next *Shipwrecked* programme, I'd be ready to go. But on my own. Or,' he adds with a wink, 'maybe with Malia…'

15

SIMON
ROGERS

Age: 23
Profession: TV company runner
Luxury Item: Fishing kit

Looking at it one way, Simon's selection for *Shipwrecked* was more or less a matter of getting there by default, as the replacement for Pierre in the event that the Frenchman's injuries might prevent him from going. On the other hand, and given how many thousands of people had applied for the trip, the fact that he was chosen as a replacement, was evidence enough that he'd satisfied the selectors that he was up to the job. He recalls:

> The selection weekend was great up until the last day, when it started to become apparent that everyone I'd bonded with kept getting eliminated. Plus, I'd had a heavy night before, so I was a bit dazed and confused. And to top it off, I didn't even know if I would be going or not. The programme-makers told me they'd keep me updated, though, and just before the departure date I got a call asking if they could come round to shoot more footage of me to go with the Selection Weekend programme. So this film crew came round, I opened the door, and there

was Andi Peters with a bottle of champagne! I couldn't believe it!

At that time, Simon jokingly referred to himself as 'the reject', although behind the humour he felt genuinely unsure as to how he stood within the group as a result of his last-minute entry:

> I was excited but apprehensive. I honestly didn't know how the others were going to respond to my being there. The worst thing was when we met at Heathrow, and the film crew wanted to keep me as a sort of surprise element. I was really scared that I'd walk out there and people would think, 'Oh it's Simon, and not Pierre.' I was really worried that they'd reject me before I'd even gotten on the plane. But when I walked round the corner they were all cheering and everything — it was a nice feeling, and from that moment on it was fine.

Simon's sense of humour (he describes himself as a 'lovable rogue') first reared its head at '*Shipwrecked* Customs', when all the group's baggage was inspected by the crew to check that no one was trying to smuggle anything onto the island. A fair amount of make-up was taken away from the British girls, and Salvo's collection of discarded tools — hammer heads and so forth — were also confiscated. Then they came to Simon's bag. As Allan wrote in his diary: 'Simon had obviously put a lot of thought into this — I know he was hoping the bags would be checked at Heathrow for maximum effect. The crew tipped the bag open. Everything was just covered in glitter. Shining elephants, giraffes, lions, hearts, circles, stars, squares all went flying all over the place. A furry claw-glove came out, a toy zebra, a pop-up fake tin of peanuts… Useless stuff. Comedy stuff. Trust me, it was funny.'

Customs eventually passed, the castaways headed for the island, as Simon recalls:

> The boat dropped us off at the shoreline so we had to get wet to actually reach the island. When we got there, all soaking wet from jumping into the sea, everyone immediately started running up the mountain, and I was like, 'Come on, let's get sorted out first, put some dry clothes on, get the ground area sorted out.' They were like a pack of wolves or a hungry bunch of kids at lunchtime – I just thought, 'I'm in the wrong place here.' Don't get me wrong, I wanted to explore the place, but there was stuff that needed to be established first. But the first night, you had Chloe-Jane, the group leader, announcing that if the programme-makers didn't give us rice, she was going to go home – it's not really what you want to hear from a leader, is it?

Having only seen a few episodes of *Shipwrecked* in the past, Simon had been pretty enthusiastic about what awaited him in Yaukuvelevu, prior to the trip. 'On the few occasions that I watched the show, I just remember seeing a lot of scantily clad women on a beach,' he had laughed. 'The only thing missing was lager. And I'm sure there's some way I can ferment some kind of alcohol over there. I've done some research, and there's this plant you can use that only grows in the South Pacific islands. I'm sorry, but I really do need my alcohol.'

And it was this fondness for alcohol that – more so than any worries about how he'd been selected – would later dictate Simon's relationship with the group, as Randy's chapter illustrates. It was an issue that actually first emerged en route to the island, as Allan recalled in his diary:

On the flight to Fiji, Simon was determined to get drunk on the free alcohol being offered around. He managed about twelve cans of lager on the first flight, wiping out the stock on two drinks trollies – in the end, they had to go and fetch supplies from the first-class cabin. I couldn't see the point myself. Of all the rubbish places to be drunk! What can you do if you're drunk, squashed up in economy class on an Air New Zealand flight? Nothing. It made me worry a bit.

Allan's concerns were echoed by Jeffro. 'Simon started out fine,' he points out. 'I remembered him from the selection weekend and I really liked him. But you know these people – and you do get them – who when they've had a drink, just want to be outrageous, they wanna prove themselves to everyone? He did it at the selection weekend, got into an argument about racism, and then, when the Americans and Australians joined us on the island, we all had a drink and he just got a bit reckless.'

That event having already been documented (again, see Randy's chapter for the full gory details), it's more important to note the effect that the evening would have on Simon's behaviour for the remainder of his stay on Yaukuvelevu. As Allan explained, 'It really had an impact on how Simon behaved for the rest of the time. He was definitely embarrassed by it all – he'd picked a fight with some-one smaller than himself and had been put on his backside straight away. And male egos being what they are, it wounded him a bit. I think he was a) worried that he'd embarrassed himself, and b) that he wouldn't be able to fulfil the role he normally played at home.'

That last observation proved to be astute, and one that Simon would later confirm himself. 'You suddenly realize that you're being presented to people on TV and they'll be watching everything you do,' he reflected, on returning to England. 'So I was constantly beating myself up over that. As far as I could see, I had two ways of approaching it — either I could do what my mates would expect me to do and be the crazy person, causing trouble and so on, or be the Simon my parents and grandparents would like to think of — Mr. Sensible, Mr Mature. So I was sort of torn between the two of them.'

Jeffro had also noticed this shift in Simon's personality: 'After that incident with Randy, he was just trying to play catch-up. He couldn't get on with people after that — people were a bit "Oh, Simon's a mentalist, watch out for that one", and so on. They got a bit wary of him. And that must have hurt him. How embarrassing must that have been? Especially with the cameras about. All the way through, though, he just couldn't get on with people. The Americans and the Australians in particular.'

The multinational element to this series of *Shipwrecked* was something that Simon had described as 'a recipe for disaster, really. I personally get on with most people,' he stressed, 'and I've been to New York, and spent a year in Australia, but it's just different cultures, isn't it? The British are very patriotic, too, so you step on that and you overstep the mark.' And there was one American in particular who failed to impress him:

Shawn was *such* a knob. He used to come over when I was building and tell me what I ought to have done here and there, and I just thought, come on, I'm building a hut that has to last for a couple of months, I don't care about the bloody double glazing. He wouldn't stop moaning about nutrition and going on about protein and carbohydrates — and I'm sorry, but he's not a doctor, you know what I mean? Rainbow was a hard worker, but so slow she might as well have been going backwards. They weren't the Americans we expected, put it that way.

And if the Americans failed to impress, then it's only fair to point out that a certain Sicilian didn't fare much better in Simon's estimation:

> With Salvo, you get the impression that he hasn't made many good friends in life, and he was the only one in that respect who didn't mind fully embarrassing himself on camera. So everyone was laughing at him, or with him, and it just encouraged him to do it more. Back here I'd have knocked him out, to be honest. He was just downright rude. He'd keep saying, 'I'm passionate, I'm Sicilian,' but that doesn't excuse anything – you don't talk to people like that.
>
> There was one morning when I was setting off to explore the island a bit, and Salvo came up and asked if he could come with me. And he was already irritating me by then. He didn't have a shirt on, so I just led him straight along the beach and into the densest forest I could find, right through the bamboo plantation. And for about three weeks after that you couldn't see his skin for the cuts he got that day. That was my little 'get back at him' thing.

For the most part, Simon was a quiet presence on the island. And then, on Day 37, he finally got his chance to make himself heard, when he was elected leader:

> I took my dad's advice – he said, 'Don't be a leader too early on, let someone else make the mistakes first.' So for the first five weeks, I just got my head down and got on with what I needed to do. Didn't really want to get involved in anything, just enjoyed myself in my own way. When I finally got voted in as leader, I came across as a bit of a dictator, but I had a lot of reasons for doing it that way. I got up

there with good intentions, trying to sort out some of the conniving, and stop Leon from bullying people. See, I already knew from Geordie that Leon was planning to escape, and now Leon was suddenly very keen to kill the pig, just so that he could enjoy some nice food before skipping off. And I thought, 'Sod that, mate, you are *not* taking my food away from me.' It sort of amounted to theft in my book, and that's something I just won't put up with.

It was with the best of intentions, then, that Simon took a firm hold on the group, although it's fair to say that his style was hardly appreciated. 'I was very aggressive, I suppose,' he admits, 'and the next day, all the people I liked actually lost their faith in me. What annoyed me was that they didn't come up and talk to me about it – I had to go and ask them what was wrong. And once I explained, they were all right – it had just all come out wrong at the meeting, and I should have addressed it much better, really.'

To add to that problem, it was also the week of the on/off/on again/off again ration run debacle. Chloe-Jane recalls this as one of the few moments when she really lost her cool on Yaukuvelevu:

On the first attempt at the ration run, Simon, who'd never been out on a boat before, wanted to start rowing to this other island in gale-force conditions. I told him it was ridiculous to even try and he wasn't having any of it. It was the week he was leader, but he just kept ranting and raving, and eventually I just erupted, and said, 'Simon, you're a complete ******.' I can't remember the exact words I used, but I just tried to give him a few home truths and there was a lot of swearing involved as well.

For his part, Simon concedes, 'I can't believe I even got involved in that ration run. It was horrible, and I'm really dreading it coming out on TV.'

Allan also had been troubled by Simon's leadership technique:

I'd been leader the week before Simon, and I didn't want to boss anyone around, I wanted to let everybody have their say. He took the exact opposite approach, dictating it all, announcing the group policies and saying that everyone had to fit in with them. He had a very different idea of what being group leader entailed. I felt that it was your role to let everyone have their say and to make sure that no one bullied a meeting. He kind of thought that it was his role to bully everyone else, and used to shout at everyone – I don't honestly think he realized what a dipstick he was being. But then, having been so quiet for so long, I think he wanted to make a big bang, and that came in the form of his leadership blitz.

In fact, Simon had already had doubts abut staying on the island, well before the ration run even occurred. 'I actually got jealous when Al, the *Shipwrecked Extra* presenter, came on the island,' he admits. 'I know how stupid that sounds, but I think it was because he was getting to do just what we were doing, only without the harsher side of it. I just thought, "What am I doing here? I'm beating myself up, I'm not being myself – what's the point in me being here? I actually went up to Al and said, "Look mate, I need to have a chat", and I had a real heart-to-heart with him, and he put me straight.'

But it was the ration run that proved to be the final straw for Simon. He got to Dravuni with Randy, Chloe-Jane and Sarah-Jane, and immediately decided not to return to Yaukuvelevu. 'We got over to Fiji and the people there were wonderful,' he recalls. 'So much love and friendship there, and they had so little to give, but they gave it all. And that was it, I just thought, "I'm not going back – I've done the survival bit, I've proved I can do it." I made a decision, actually – if I'd gone back, it would have been to cause trouble – you know, loosening structures, that kind of thing, just messing about. But I thought, no, there's no need for that.'

Looking back on the experience, Simon feels that he had no real expectations to fulfil:

I never really followed *Shipwrecked*, so I approached it with no real preconceptions. I didn't really ask any questions about it in advance – I thought we'd have to do tasks for food or something like that. I certainly didn't realize it was going to be so boring. Don't get me wrong, I'm so grateful I went to Fiji – it's something I'll never get to do again. Sure, it could have been a bit better, with different people there and without the cameras, but it was definitely an experience.

And true to form, his return to England followed a set pattern: 'When I got back,' he grins, 'I just got completely drunk. Two of my best mates met me at the airport, I went back home, slung my bag in, then went out drinking and didn't come home for four days. I must have been drunk for ninety-odd hours.' Simon wouldn't deny the changes that the Yaukuvelevu experience brought about in him, however: 'I've learned something, but it's hard to put a finger on it. In my environment back here with my mates I'm very different, more in control... I'm certainly used to being heard, I suppose. I went into *Shipwrecked* thinking that people would listen, but I soon found out that you have to prove yourself first before they will.'

16

RAINBOW-SHALOM
JOHNSON

Age: 23
Profession: Aspiring actress
Luxury Item: Drum

Having already appeared in short films and commercials, Rainbow was, if anything, the media veteran of the *Shipwrecked* cast. But like the other Americans, she had very little idea of what to expect from the show. 'A few weeks before I set off, I was freaking out,' she admits, 'because the closest thing to this we have in America is *Survivor*, and that's very harsh, with people starving and competing. I thought that was what it would be like, you know, having to hunt for food and so on. Then I managed to get hold of a tape of *Shipwrecked 2*, and I really relaxed – it seemed like they were having a lot of fun. It looked like MTV's *The Real World*, only set on an island.'

At the American selection weekend, the crew had been struck by Rainbow's peaceful demeanour, describing her as 'generally likeable in a cool, "girl-next-door" kind of way', and adding that she 'comes out with quite a lot of Californian new-agey stuff'. Rainbow confirms this, saying 'I'm a little out there – I'm a weird, spiritual person, that's how I was raised. I'm really looking forward to being on this island, with a new family, away from industry and technology and seeing what we make of it. I want to reconnect with nature. I'm so excited – so ready for this.'

Unsurprisingly, Rainbow felt that the international aspect of the show was a very positive element, and one that she embraced:

> I don't really feel very nationalistic, to be honest. I was raised to feel fortunate for being born wherever you were born. But being picked, and being the only American woman, then you do get the feeling of being a representative. But as far as I'm concerned, the more diverse the group, the better. And let's face it, anyone who wanted to do this would have to be pretty amazing.

Possibly the most enthusiastic member of the group before she set off, Rainbow had just the two concerns. Firstly, like Malia, she is a vegetarian. That, though, was something she'd happily rationalized before embarking on the trip: 'Vegetarianism is a luxury and a choice when you can choose what you eat,' she points out, 'and I have been trying to eat fish, just so that I wouldn't freak out. It's going to be awesome. I just hope that my body can take whatever I have to eat.' The second worry? 'I have no real knowledge of survival, so I'm a little concerned what I can bring to the group.'

It wasn't long, then, before Rainbow's *Real World* vision was shattered, and the reality of the experience became a wholly different prospect. 'Well, it turned out to be *Survivor*, didn't it?' she admits, laughing. 'Only without the money prize at the end of it! When I tell people I went to Fiji, their faces light up and I have to tell them that it wasn't "romantic honeymoon Fiji", but "Nightmare hell Fiji". It was genuinely shocking to see people hungry – I'm never going to forget how hungry we were in the first two weeks.'

The effects of the new, tougher regime were immediately apparent, and demanded a rethink on Rainbow's part:

> It's unfortunate. I had all these plans for bonding games, just things that would unite the group, but I gave up on that pretty early on when I realized that the different personalities were just too strong. There was an automatic resistance to that. Besides, from the moment we arrived, we really had to work our butts off to make sure we had food. So at the end of the day we were just exhausted, and didn't have any energy to do anything other than sleep.

As everyone else on the island confirms, Rainbow soon set about making herself useful on a practical level. Having worried about what skills she might bring to the island, she immediately demonstrated perhaps one of the most necessary qualities of all for such a testing experience: the willingness to get your head down and get stuff done. 'It's my nature and my heritage to work hard for a group,' she explains. 'It's just the way I've been raised. I was amazed to see the British girls sunbathing when we got there – I'd ask if they'd help to weave some leaves for the shelters and they were like, "Oh no, I can't be bothered." And that attitude, that "Can't be bothered" approach, is very polite, but very acidic at the same time. But,' she shrugs, 'you can't make someone work if they don't want to.'

Rainbow, though, wanted to work. And hardly stopped, the whole time she was on Yaukuvelevu. 'In fact,' she says, 'the only time that I let things really get me down on the island was after I cut my finger open, because I wasn't able to work. And when you're not able to work on that island and keep yourself busy, it's a bit of a bummer. And I think everyone who got hurt out there felt the same way – it's not easy to have other people pulling your weight for you.'

As you can imagine, with such a firm belief in the communal ideal, Rainbow's response to the news that people on the island had been serving themselves before others came as a heavy blow. 'I felt so shocked when I heard about people stealing from the group,' she says, 'I mean, we all knew we were coming to the island, and that we had to look after each other. I was kinda surprised to see that not everyone had the same idea.' Those comments immediately call to mind the early problems with Genevieve. Rainbow abstained in the expulsion vote, and offers an alternative theory as to a possible reason behind the eviction:

The main thing with Genevieve was that she didn't have the bikini, if you know what I mean. Maybe the guys just weren't sexually attracted to her, and I feel like that played a part, however small, in why that all happened. Just because the other girls were prettier didn't mean that they were innocent. Genevieve and I bonded – I always had a warm feeling from her… It was a pity that she did have that side to her, where she harboured things, kept a little tucked to one side. But at the same time, I didn't like the idea of the group being in control of one person's destiny. That incident shifted everything for me because from that moment on, I didn't have any trust for those people any more. I was just disappointed that we could do this so soon, and in such a bad way. After someone's been 'executed' like that, it's hard to be open and trusting in the same way.

The failings of the island community troubled Rainbow throughout the stay and she was quick to identify the root of the problem. 'In an American show I think they'd have given the group special tasks to accomplish together, just ways of creating a group dynamic,' she explains, 'but we had none of those, we were just on our own, creating our *own* tasks, I suppose. But they weren't for fun, they were to survive.'

As the rose-tinted glasses came off, Rainbow found her own way of dealing with the constant arguing and bickering in the camp. And while many of the other castaways felt that she was withdrawing into herself, the simple fact was that – faced with an experience that was being tainted by hostile elements – she was simply finding a way of making that experience *hers* again:

> I think I idealized a little bit about how it would be, but any time there was a fight, I'd go up on a hill and look up to the clouds or the stars, and that really helped me at the times when it seemed like chaos and battle were the only things that people were interested in. You know, I was really looking forward to getting away from the daily politics of city living, but it seemed that the politics followed us to the island. And I do have a strong sense of justice, but I was thinking, 'Should I really get involved here and try to straighten things out?' Because when you've got people like Salvo being so messed up in such a loud way, there's just no point in getting involved.

And so Rainbow's retreats became an essential a part of her ongoing survival strategy:

> I don't know exactly what propelled me to do that. Maybe it was Randy saying something racist, or Salvo saying something hurtful, but I just realized I didn't want to be these people's teacher, especially since they weren't ready to learn anything. I just needed to go off on my own, and I don't fully understand why. I actually spent a few nights on a very windy peak, walking in the dark without a lantern –

I definitely shut myself off. I felt there were already enough people offering their opinions, and no one was listening to them anyway, so why would I want to just be another voice?

Rainbow admits she found one aspect of her period as a castaway particularly frustrating: the fact that a small group of people had shared ten weeks together without really getting to know each other. And in particular, she felt hurt that the majority of her fellow shipwreckees showed little interest in finding out more about her:

> I'm fascinated by people and I ask a lot of questions, and I could tell you *so* much about the families of the people out there, their relationships with their loved ones. But by the same token, I didn't feel like anyone asked me a question once, which was bizarre. And when I got back home and people started asking me about the trip, I was like, 'Wow, you want to ask *me* something?' It just seemed like ages since anyone had been truly interested in anything I had to say. Malia and Geordie were the only people I could have a proper conversation with out there. Thank *God* for Malia, that's all I have to say. She has a great head on her shoulders. She helped me to feel sane throughout it, and she was so much fun as well. We actually talked about starting our own community at one point, just making our way to another island for a few nights, but ultimately I didn't want to create another division.

That said, there were friendships to be made outside of the group as well, and Rainbow soon found a new set of friends on the island. 'I would hang out with the boatmen at night, watching the sunsets, just chilling,' she smiles:

They'd secretly help me build stuff and tell me where to find more lemon trees and so on. And one of them said he'd bring me some peanuts, and I said, 'No, really, we'll get some when we go on the ration run,' because they don't earn that much. But he didn't listen, and the next day, down by the coconut tree was this tin of peanuts. I was so amazed. I called a secret meeting without the camera crew knowing anything about it, and everyone got so defensive, wanting to know what it was all about. I said, 'You know what, just chill out and enjoy the surprise.' So we managed to sneak away to a beach and passed out the nuts. And it was such a small quantity, but it was like gold to us. And he even brought a second tin a few days later; it was so sweet of him.

But perhaps unsurprisingly, even such a gesture of kindness could be soured by the tensions within the group. Rainbow's insistence on absolute fairness meant that the peanuts were to be counted out individually and shared among them all. Allan, having upset her earlier that day, tried to make amends by taking on that chore. Unfortunately, some other members of the group found the sight of him counting out peanuts rather more amusing than he did. 'I was sat there counting these peanuts out,' he laughs, 'thinking, "I can't believe I'm doing this." And Salvo just wouldn't let go of the fact that I was counting out these bloody peanuts. I suppose half of my anger was in the fact that I didn't want to be doing this anyway, so I ended up having a go at him – if the table hadn't been between us, I'd have probably lamped him.'

We've already seen in Randy's chapter how some of the male focus on the appearance of the females had upset Rainbow, and this subject would recur during the course of the stay:

Tonight, after dinner, Salvo said that he would sooner die than sleep with anyone on the island. Then he started gossiping at the top of his voice about all these supposed torrid affairs that people were having on the island, affairs that simply didn't exist. As a finishing touch, he rated the girls in order of attractiveness, with Malia first, Vicki second, Chloe-Jane third, Sarah-Jane fourth, and myself last. So once again, I'm made to feel unattractive. I can't help wondering if this is some kind of test. I didn't think I was that bad, and it's a comment from Salvo, whom *no one* finds attractive.

But to balance out these lows, there were equally memorable highs, and Rainbow doesn't hesitate to point to one very special night. Now, the event in question is one that is best filed under 'You had to be there to fully understand', but it's one that all present commented on in their diaries, all with the same sense of quiet amazement:

It was one of those moments where you had just the right group of people. I just said, 'Hey, does anyone want to come down and watch the moon from the beach?' and Jeffro, Chloe-Jane and Malia all said yes, so we just picked up a lantern and found ourselves walking towards the beach to watch the moon over the sea. We were standing there hugging side by side, looking up at this amazing sky. The sight was breathtaking, it really was. And all around it was almost totally silent — just the sound of water lapping against the sand. And just at that moment, when we really felt like the luckiest people on earth, this lantern started to make this weird howling sound — we'd never heard anything like it, and we'd certainly never heard a lantern making any noise in all our time on the island. Everybody got spooked out, but it was just a special situation, one that we all attached our own special meaning to. It was almost as though our loved ones were calling us in this situation where we had no means of communication.

A definite 'moment', then, and Rainbow admits that there were many such times, her only regret being that the true beauty of them only became fully clear when she arrived back home. 'It's only now when I pull back from the experience that I'm fully aware of just how beautiful that island was. When you're *in* that experience, it's pretty difficult to appreciate everything that's around you,' she confirms. I know people are going to watch the show and they'll be amazed by how beautiful Yaukuvelevu is — every scene's going to look gorgeous. But as a small speck on that island, it seems different somehow. I just tried to keep my eyes open to it all, to explore and appreciate the place.'

In her appraisal of the Yaukuvelevu experience, Rainbow has weighed up many of the changes it's brought about in her outlook on life and on people. 'I've been through a lot in my life,' she says, 'and hard as this experience was, this wasn't the worst situation I've ever had to confront. In a way it was unpleasant, because not everything is as happy, lovey-dovey and idealized as you might want it to be — if it had been a group of people who'd wanted to go out there and get along, as opposed to just being on television, it would have been a different story. I think all our focuses were very different.'

And quite surprisingly in light of her profession, she points to the camera as one of the negative elements of her time on the island:

As an actress, I found that it really changed my relationship with the camera, just seeing the way that people allowed it to dictate the way they behaved. And it's very weird having your day-to-day life documented. When I got back to LA, I felt some resistance to the camera and found myself thinking, 'I don't want to be an actress any more.' But then an advert that I'd filmed before *Shipwrecked* started airing just as I got back and I just thought, 'You know, I'm going to keep trying. I'm not going to kill myself over this, but I'll stick with it.'

There's an underlying optimism to Rainbow, an insistence on focusing on the positive at all times, and it becomes crystal clear when she sums up her thoughts on the experience. You could call it hippy-dippy if you're one for pigeonholing people, but it's hard to fault the spirit behind it:

Hopefully everyone has a spirit that wants to gain positive things from life, so I think most everybody there wanted to shine and get into an upward spiral. There was no monetary gain involved, obviously, so what you actually earned from the experience was down to the individual – but I think every single person worked so hard to get something out of it, and we certainly took away an appreciation for the little things in life. And that's a big thing to gain. I thought I already had that capacity, but I have it to the gazillionth degree now, I truly do.

17

SALVATORE 'SALVO' RIGGI

Age: 23
Profession: Waiter
Luxury Item: None

Now, you might have assumed, and not unreasonably, that the cruellest challenge faced by the *Shipwrecked* castaways was the lack of food rations. There are some, however, who would argue that this particular hardship paled into insignificance compared to being marooned with a nudity-prone former stripper from Sicily suffering from an apparent diplomacy-bypass. One thing, though, is absolutely certain: you have *never* in your life met anyone like Salvo.

Now based in London, Salvo tells how, as a fourteen-year-old, he was involved in a motorbike accident in his home country of Sicily. A collision with a car left him in a coma for six days, and he views his subsequent survival as a miracle, adding that it explains why he now fears nothing. One side-effect of the accident was that he now remembers nothing of his life prior to that accident; another is the scar over his left eye.

I was a stripper in Sicily for three years. My mother wasn't happy with this, and one day I tell her, 'OK, Mama, no problem, I go to London and change my life.' So I come to London, I work as barman, as waiter, but in my blood I like television, I like films. Now, I have never seen myself on television before, but when I was eighteen years old, I tell my mother, 'Mama, Mama, I wanna work in television.' And she always tell me, 'Don't speak bullshit.' Now I am twenty-three years old, and the dream is a reality!

As early on as the selection weekend, Salvo's larger-than-life personality had already proved hard to ignore. Gemma noted not long initially meeting him, 'He really did me in. I thought, "God, if I was on an island with you, I'd actually end up killing you!" I called him Darius, 'cos I didn't know his real name, and he looked like that bloke out of *Popstars*. The guy is so loud! He was the one person [at the selection weekend] that I wasn't too sure about – I can see a few ups and downs happening with him.'

Before heading off to Yaukuvelevu, Salvo had given a great deal of thought to the possibility of those ups and downs and arrived at the conclusion that, 'The most important quality on the island, if you're gonna stay there ten weeks, is to live in peace with people. If you are kind with them, they are kind with you. If you respect people, I think you get respect back.' Now this might seem somewhat at odds with the man you've already read about in the preceding chapters, a man who managed to have an argument with every single person on the island at one time or another, but then consistency is possibly not the quality you'd most immediately associate with Salvo.

That said, and as all the castaways would readily agree, for all his faults (and there was, as you'll see shortly, a very long list of those), Salvo also had his good points. He was universally considered the best cook on the island, an accolade he accepted proudly:

'Food is the most important thing in the world,' he beamed. 'I love cooking for people. I like cooking for myself as well, but if people are with me I want them to have nice food also – I like them to be happy.'

Quite usefully, Salvo also appointed himself chief slaughterer of livestock on Yaukuvelevu, although it's worth noting that there was hardly stiff competition for the job:

> I decided that I would be the killer of the beasts, because the other people were a little scared. But I wanted to kill the pig – maybe it's because I'm Sicilian, from a different culture, I wanted to try it. But believe me, when I plunged the knife in its throat I felt very bad. My heart was so small, because I saw the pig's eyes. But my life was more impor-tant than the pig's, you know? Afterwards, everybody enjoyed the pig, but I will always remember in my heart the noise the pig made and the look in its eyes.

As far as the lack of rations was concerned, Salvo – while he may have complained as much as the others of being hungry while on the island – insists now that it didn't trouble him. 'I'm a clever person,' he claims. 'If I was hungry, I went to look for coconuts. See, if you are a clever person, you find food. If you are lazy, though, if you just sit on the beach getting your suntan, then you are going to be in trouble, because your stomach gets small.'

Which might sound like a reference to certain parties in the group, although Salvo is quick to insist that communal life on the island was like being a part of one big, happy family. 'Everybody on the island was nice,' he gushes. 'I liked everybody there, I don't know why, it's perhaps because my heart is so big. That's why I like everybody. I like all people in the world. That's why I am here in the world, because I like them so much!'

This, you'll recall, is the man who liked Donna so much he rejoiced in telling her she was fat (point of fact: she isn't); the man who liked Genevieve so much that he urged Leon to be 'aggressive! Like a pitbull!' when chairing the meeting that would lead to her expulsion; the man who liked Rainbow so much he slipped obscene notes into her diary. Plainly, Salvo's recollection of what happened on Yaukuvelevu is not quite the same as that of his fellow castaways.

And it's to them that we turn for a clearer picture of the man. While everyone saw the good in him, they also experienced the not-so-good, and from an uncomfortably close proximity, as well. American Shawn, who came close to exchanging blows with Salvo, is a good an example of the mixed feelings that surround the Sicilian. 'I respect him for the way he was brought up,' Shawn stresses immediately. 'He raised himself, basically, and he educated himself, and you have to respect that. But on the other hand, there's no avoiding the fact that he had no tact at all, and in a situation like the one we were in, that was a real problem. I mean, if you want something from someone, you don't call them a fat bitch, like he did with Donna.'

Shawn also pointed to the problem of Salvo's attitude towards the female members of the group, although stressing that the problem was partly of the girls' making:

He'd be groping and hugging the girls and they'd just say, 'Oh, that's just the way he is.' But as soon as he started *verbally* insulting people, they didn't make the same kind of allowance – they'd get upset and say that it was wrong. Well hello, it's also wrong when he grabs your tits! I'll be honest with you, if it had been back home I would have ripped his throat out if I saw him doing that to a girl. It's something I've never tolerated. But what really disappointed me the most was the other people's reactions. If you're going to yell at him for being obnoxious, then yell at him for groping as well – that was what confused him and caused a lot of the conflicts. People decided to accept certain aspects of his behaviour on a selective basis, and that made things difficult.

As we heard in an earlier chapter, Rainbow had already been on the receiving end of this kind of disrespect from Salvo, but even when she returned home, he still managed to keep cropping up in her thoughts

> When I got back to LA, I kept going on about this Sicilian guy who'd been so horrible, although I was actually still wearing a necklace he'd made for me. My little cousin said, 'Rainbow, why are you keeping that on? Isn't it unlucky?' and I thought she was absolutely right, so I cut it off and it felt good. Salvo was the hardest person for me to process out of all of them. He was constantly exposing himself, he would terrorize us into letting him cook, and swindle extra food for himself in the process. He was the worst stealer and *such* a child. He was very powerful, very judgmental. Being subjected to Salvo was definitely one of the hardest aspects of it all.

Allan, as one of the castaways whom Salvo genuinely liked, is a little more charitable in his views. He even goes as far as to say that if he were to repeat the *Shipwrecked* experience, Salvo would be one of the people he'd want to take with him:

> I loved him and I hated him. But in the end, he's so infectious. There were things about him that really annoyed me out there. I thought that a lot of his behaviour was just for

the camera's benefit, but I've met up with him since I've been back in England, and he's even more over the top without the cameras. It's just him. He's unbelievable. But I do hope he's the only Salvo in the world. I can't imagine there being another one, to be honest.

Allan also points up some of Salvo's gifts – such as the fact that he could turn his hand to almost anything, that he learned quickly and that the phrase 'I can't be bothered' didn't enter into his vocabulary.

His English, when we got to the island was really terrible, and he got very frustrated and very angry really easily, because he just couldn't get across what he needed to do. So he'd just start shouting, and a lot of people took a very negative view of that, myself included. But he's got one of those fantastic linguistic minds, whereby he hears a word once, and immediately remembers it, and how to use it. And his English just got so much better. He'd never written the language before, but that didn't stop him writing a diary.

Unsurprisingly, Salvo is quick to confirm this: 'Of *course* my English is better,' he grins, 'I have been on an island for three months and I speak with English, with Australians, with Americans. I'm English now!'

But even Allan found that there were moments when Salvo was a little more than human patience could cope with, as he explains:

I always said before I went out there that I wasn't going to let things bother me, and to a greater extent I succeeded. I exploded twice. At Salvo. One time was the business with the peanuts that I was sharing out for Rainbow, the other was when Shawn was trying to light a fire and not having much luck with it, and Salvo was just shouting at him. Which was ridiculous – you don't have a go at someone who's trying. I tried to explain that to Salvo, but he wasn't having any of it and just shouted more, but he still kept going on – eventually I just yelled, 'SHUT YOUR FACE!' There was a camera there, so I didn't want to swear, even though I really wanted to there and then. But five minutes later he came and found me and apologized, and we were walking back to camp arms around each other.

Even Pierre, in the short time he spent on the island, was highly aware of the Sicilian: 'Salvo is a really strange man,' he grins. 'After Leon left he was totally different. I actually think Leon controlled him a lot. It was funny, though – Salvo was always accusing people of being two-faced, and yet he was the most two-faced person on that island. On camera he was always friendly and nice, but when the cameras left he was always arguing.'

The most frequently made comment about Salvo, though, is the fact that he appeared to have only one true love on the island – namely the camera. Every day he would record 'The Salvo Show', and indeed, on returning to England, he announced, 'my plan now is to be an actor. I'd like to have a television show, "The Salvo Show", in which I interview people. There are so many things I could do!'

While few of the castaways saw any immediate TV future opening up for Salvo, he did, at least, provide one of the island's finest comedy moments, as Allan confirms:

By far and away the funniest thing that happened out there won't get shown on TV because there wasn't a camera around to capture it. Salvo's fire-dancing. It was the funniest thing ever. Like I said, the guy picks things up so incredibly quickly – he'd never played much football in England, but was immediately doing headers with Jeffro. Plus, he also gets drunk really quickly. So when he saw Malia's fire-twiddling bits after a couple of beers, he suddenly launched one into the air and caught it. Malia said, 'That's incredible, I've never seen anyone pick it up so fast.'

So immediately, Salvo decides he has to go one better, whips off his shorts, and is now completely naked, and starts throwing the fire-sticks about again, but spinning them around his legs. They're attached to chains, so he put the chain in his mouth and started spinning around like a helicopter up and down the beach. He must have done it for 45 seconds or so, then, inevitably, he fell over and he'd put so much lighter fluid on it that the flames shot up over his knees to his groin. Engulfed it. My eyes were streaming by then. Honestly, I've never laughed so much. Next morning, I ask him, 'So Salvo, how are you?', and he says, 'Oh Allan – I have burned my dick.' You know what? I just cannot imagine that island without Salvo. The show may as well be called *Salvo-wrecked* as far as I'm concerned.

Back in England, Salvo – even if his memory of events doesn't quite tally with that of the others – is an unstoppably happy and excited man. 'I think *Shipwrecked* and Yaukuvelevu is the best experience of my life,' he says. 'Now I appreciate everything: I appreciate food, I appreciate people. I feel different inside now, because I took some great experiences away from the island, and they will stay in my heart for the rest of my life. It's an experience that happens only once in your life, and it happened to me so I am a very lucky man.'

But there remains one regret for him, namely the fact that he was never elected group leader on the island. 'The only bad moment for my heart was in the last week,' he frowns, 'because that is when I was supposed to be leader. The other people voted for Jeffro, because Chloe-Jane had told people not to vote for me. And I found that some people say one thing, but do another. They told me that they would vote for me, and I believed them.' Pressed on this, he identifies Sarah-Jane as one of the culprits: 'She only worked hard for one week,' he claims, 'because she wanted my vote for leader. After I gave her my vote, she didn't give her vote to me and she became a lazy person again. And I did not appreciate Simon, either,' he adds. 'He's a good person and a good worker, but sometimes when he drinks he's not polite, and I don't like that very much. Some people were not honest – some people were liars when the camera was there.'

As the chef of the island, Salvo was a master of improvisation (in the least conducive of circumstances), and it's only natural that the first thing on his mind when he got to London was food. 'The first meal when I got back was so beautiful,' he beams:

I fried onions, bacon, Parma ham and Mortadella, all finely chopped, then I added some cooked pasta and two eggs. I scrambled it all together like a carbonara. My stomach was so full. You know what? I've changed a lot now. Before, for example, I would buy a pizza, eat half of it and throw the other half away. Now, I put the other half in the fridge for the next day. And when I go to bed I think about Yaukuvelevu. Every night. I can't forget it. I want to do it all again, but for six months this time, and only me on the island. For me, the best moment was every day, every single second, everything. Even the bad days were a good experience.

ISLAND
'CONSTITUTION'

1   Once a week the group will hold a meeting where all 17 contributors MUST attend. The first meeting will take place on the day of arrival on the island, before dark. The second meeting will take place two or three days later on a day to be specified by the production, and then weekly from then on. The group is free to hold additional meetings as and when they desire. The group must give a minimum of 15 minutes notice to the production team of any group meeting.

2   At the weekly meeting, the group will elect, or re-elect a leader for the following week. Anyone making a nomination must explain why an individual should become leader. One person, one vote, the winner is the person with the most votes, in the case of a draw the two tied candidates will draw lots.

3   The previously elected leader will act as chairman at these meetings, and must ensure that everybody gets their chance to speak, each in turn, and not all at once.

4   Each member of the group is bound to follow the leader's decisions. If, at any point during the week, they are unwilling to do

so, then the matter will be put to the rest of the group and the majority decision will be binding.

5 The group will be given two cameras with which to film themselves. One of these cameras (hutcam) will be secured in a secluded area away from the camp to provide complete privacy. Each member of the group must visit this camera at least once a week to record some of their thoughts. It is fundamental that members of the group respect each other's privacy whilst using this facility. The camera will be fixed in such a way that no one will be able to view another person's footage or record over it. The group will be trained how to use the second camera themselves. Anyone in the group is allowed to use this camera to shoot anything they want during the ten weeks on the understanding that the material shot belongs to the production and may well be used in the final programmes.

6 Castaways can leave the island on compassionate grounds. Compassionate grounds are: health problems (mental or physical to be diagnosed by a doctor), and bad news from back home (which will be relayed by the production). In any case they must first seek the permission of the production team by approaching hutcam. The production team will then brief the leader who will be obliged to hold a meeting and inform the group. (Such permission to leave on compassionate grounds will not be unreasonably withheld.).

7 Voluntarily leaving the island: Should someone wish to leave the island, they must first approach hutcam and put forward their nomination. The production team will then brief the leader who is obliged to hold a meeting and inform the group. There must be a simple majority in favour for the nomination

to succeed. Should the person be successful they must leave the island the following morning at 7.00am. As a forfeit the person leaving the island must comply with a rice penalty, whereby an unspecified amount of the group's rice will be confiscated and removed from the island with the castaway.

8 Compulsory expulsion from the island: If an individual or individuals want to propose the expulsion of another member of the group they must make their nomination to hutcam. The production team will then brief the leader who will then be obliged to present the proposal to the group at a meeting. The individual in question must be given an opportunity to defend himself/herself before the rest of the group vote on the final decision. The voting will be done by secret ballot and there must be a majority of votes in favour for the expulsion to be carried out. The production team will not divulge the identity of the nominator to the group whilst the group remain on the island. The expelled individual will leave the island at 7.00am the following morning. If collaboration or connivance is discovered between the expellee and the rest of the group then the vote will be deemed null and void.

9 If anyone is expelled or leaves the island before the end of the project, they will be put on the first available flight back to the airport of their departure. Those that stay to the end of the period may be able to delay their return flight to the airport of their departure, should they so wish.

10 The group is allowed one ration run during their period of time on the island. This is for emergency purposes. It is up to the group to decide when that takes place. A maximum of five people will be allowed on the ration run.

11 In an emergency the group are allowed one visit from Man Friday to supplement their rations. To summon Man Friday they must light a bonfire on the highest peak of the island at sunset.

12 Castaways cannot visit any other island without first seeking permission from the production team. The production team reserve the right to deny their requests.

13 Apart from the above, the group may vote additional island 'laws' as they desire, by simple majority, but these must be ratified by the production (approval not to be unreasonably withheld).

14 The producer has absolute discretion to remove any individual whose behaviour, for any reason, is deemed to threaten the success of this enterprise.